M000191743

"You're going to have fun! I
objects to introduce the G(
friends—'just like Mike.'"

—Luis Palau, author of *High Definition Life*

"Mike Silva empowers Christians with a multitude of fresh, contemporary, and clear illustrations of the Good News of Jesus Christ. Just reading them motivates me to share them with someone else. If you feel you just don't know how to share Christ with a friend or stranger, *Would You Like Fries With That?* will give you dynamic stories to make the Good News clear and compelling."

—Tim Robnett, Director, Next Generation Alliance®

"For over a decade, Mike Silva has been one of the most powerful evangelists at Promise Keepers conferences. In *Would You Like Fries With That?* Mike makes it easy for all of us to share our faith. The down-to-earth illustrations, dynamic quotations, and relevant Scriptures he relates in this book will equip you to make a vital Gospel connection with virtually anyone—and to help fulfill the Great Commission."

—Tom Fortson, President/CEO, Promise Keepers

"In many cultures, the communicator's credibility depends on his ability to evoke and tell stories that match ideas. In fact, I require my students in evangelistic preaching to present original, personal stories to illustrate the basic framework of the Good News: sin, salvation, saving faith. Mike Silva has given us a veritable treasure trove..."

—Ramesh Richard, Professor, Dallas Theological Seminary

"Mike has always been a person to tell it like he sees it. His use of personal descriptions and observations puts the truth of the kingdom into every person's terms. Mike is able to communicate to any person in any walk of life. This book and Mike's passion for the proclamation for salvation are the real deal."

—Brian W. Blomberg, Chief Development Officer,
The National Center for Fathering

"No one I know is more qualified to help the Body of Christ understand the importance of incarnating the gospel message. He personally has traveled the world doing exactly what he teaches here. Mike has taught our church what it means to reach people with love...around the corner and around the world."

—Rick Kingham, Lead Pastor, Overlake Christian Church, Seattle

"Mike Silva either has way too much time on his hands, or (more likely, because I know how busy Mike is for the Kingdom) he is just wired to take notice of all the little things in life that point to God and His love for us.   We should *all* be so wired!"

—Wayne Shepherd, Moody Broadcasting

"The truths in *Would You Like Fries With That?* will change you forever. In a world that's spiraling downwards, this little book is a parachute!"

—Phil Callaway, speaker and author of *Wonders Never Cease*

"Mike Silva is a bold, passionate, and articulate evangelist proclaiming the truth of Jesus Christ! Listening to his message of God's love for us is life changing!"

—Barbara Rosberg, Vice President, America's Family Coaches

"Compelling clarity and compassion mark the ministry of Mike Silva... The fruit of his ministry is evidence of God's hand on his life!"

—Crawford Loritts Jr., Associate Director, US Ministries, Campus Crusade for Christ

"Mike Silva radiates a passion for Jesus Christ that is powerfully contagious. His love for Christ, the Church, and the lost authenticates his gift as an evangelist. He is genuine!"

—Joseph Garlington, Senior Pastor, Covenant Church of Pittsburgh

"Mike preaches the love of God with power and passion. Jesus Christ is accurately and practically presented whenever this 'evangelist' announces the Good News of the Gospel."

—Bruce W. Fong, President, Michigan Theological Seminary

"What a great read for all of us looking for a jump-start for our hearts. Mike has put on paper both the enthusiasm and substance that I have found refreshing in his preaching."

—Dr. Joseph M. Stowell, Teaching Pastor, Harvest Bible Chapel, Rolling Hills, Illinois

"Not only does Mike Silva have a national evangelistic platform...but he has served with our team in multiple cities and pre-crusade meetings. I believe God will use him in the days ahead."

—Franklin Graham, President, Samaritan's Purse

Would You Like Fries With That?

101 WAYS TO PICTURE
THE GOOD NEWS
OF JESUS CHRIST

by Mike Silva
and Matt Williames, illustrator

PUBLISHING
SINCE 1928

Published in association with the literary agency of Sanford Communications, Inc., 6406 N.E. Pacific St., Portland, OR 97213.

ISBN 0529-12081-X

Printed in the United States of America

1 2 3 4 5—09 08 07 06 05

To Crystal, my love.

When I was a teenager and fell in love with you, I thought I knew you. However, after twenty-seven years of marriage and four sensational daughters, I know you are far more than I ever could have imagined!

The wisest man in the history of the world had you in mind when he wrote:

> She extends her hand to the poor,
> Yes, she reaches out her hands to the needy.
> She opens her mouth with wisdom,
> And on her tongue is the law of kindness.
> Her children rise up and call her blessed;
> Her husband also, and he praises her.
> Charm is deceitful and beauty is passing,
> But a woman who fears the LORD,
> she shall be praised.
> —*Proverbs 31:20, 26, 28, 30*

Who would have thought that a girl like you would fall for a guy like me? (Proof there is a God in heaven!)

ACKNOWLEDGMENTS

David Sanford, Matt Williames, Randy Elliott, and World Publishing, I shake my head when I think about the risk you have courageously taken on with someone like me. Without you, I would be like a snowboard without snow.

Bill Sands, Mike Zanon, and Jane True, don't even think about what I owe you. It's embarrassing!

Stormy Boyles, thank you for typing every word on every page. You are incredible. And my special thanks to Elizabeth Ries Jones and Elizabeth Honeycutt for polishing what I wrote.

My deep gratitude to Chris Shaffer, Dick Blair, Al Egg, Bill Light, Mike Hodges, Byron Roach, and David VanDyke. To be surrounded by a board of directors known for their wisdom, compassion for the lost, and love for me and my family, is powerful. I humbly thank you. In fact, *you* are the reason I am.

Max and Denalyn Lucado, Joseph Stowell, Luis Palau, Promise Keepers, Harry Thomas and Tim Landis (Creation Music Festivals), Drew Dickens (Need Him Radio)—each of you have put your arm around me and repeatedly encouraged, loved, and coached me. Sharing platforms, conversations, and prayer with you have been highlights for me.

Lord God Almighty, thank you for promising to be a Father to the Fatherless. I am, you are, and therefore I praise you.

CONTENTS

FOREWORD

You'll look a long time before you'll find anyone with a deeper love for Christ and people than that of Mike Silva. His twin passions have propelled him all over the world, but never too far from the heart of his bride and always in the shadow of the cross.

Every engagement I've ever had with Mike has encouraged me. Hearing him address musicians in Portland, men on a men's retreat, or the people of the Oak Hills Church in San Antonio. . . each message was meaningful and memorable.

I pray you find this book to be the same. May God use it to remind us of His highest hope—that every person be saved.

—Max Lucado

SCRIPTURE INDEX

INTRODUCTION

Imagine sitting in a restaurant enjoying a delicious meal with an unsaved friend. One glance at the ketchup bottle or the salt and pepper shakers brings a smile to your face. Why? Thanks to *Would You Like Fries With That?*, you know you can use those everyday objects to visually illustrate several important gospel truths.

Or imagine talking with a sales clerk at your favorite store. As she scans the items you wish to purchase, you open up your wallet and pull out a crisp new $20 bill. Again, you find yourself smiling. Thanks to *Would You Like Fries With That?*, you can use this opportunity to talk about each person's value to God.

All Christians have some idea of the basic beliefs of Christianity. We know that Jesus Christ is God's Son, who died on the cross, was buried, and rose on the third day to pay for our sins. We know the message, but *how* do we share it?

The secret of success in evangelism comes with understanding. As the old Chinese proverb says, "Tell me and I will forget; show me and I may remember; involve me and I will understand."

When a person can *visualize* the message of the gospel, it makes more sense! This book is a resource to help you picture God's offer of salvation when you're talking with others.

Nothing is more exciting!

USING YOUR "MAN DOWN" BUTTON

During an extensive tour of a fire station, which included a spectacular ride straight up in the air standing inside the truck's 135-foot ladder tower, I noticed a red button on the firefighter's radio.

I asked about it, and he explained that it was the "man down" button. This button is activated only in emergencies. It's reserved for highest priority situations.

When a firefighter activates the button, a signal is sent as an immediate flashing alert on the dispatch's monitor. Dispatch then breaks over the radio with priority traffic and states that they are receiving the "man down" alert from a firefighter at a specific location.

The Rapid Intervention Team is engaged immediately. The "R.I.T." is a group of highly trained individuals whose sole purpose at each fire is to rescue endangered firefighters.

The incident commander dispatches every resource of the department in the rescue process. Though the fire rages, priority is the "man down."

Heaven works in a similar way. When an individual spiritually wakes up, he realizes that the oxygen is out of his tank, the smoke is so thick in his life that visibility is zero, and the floor in the burning building has just collapsed, trapping him.

His life flashes in front of him. He realizes he is out of options.

Right then he remembers his "man down" button.

Spiritually speaking, the moment you activate your "man down" button, Jesus shows up to your rescue. You become priority. He dispatches the resources of His Heavenly Rapid Intervention Team to rescue you from sin, guilt, and all wrongdoing. His death and resurrection become your salvation.

The Bible Says:

The LORD is near to all who call upon Him, to all who call upon Him in truth.
He will fulfill the desire of those who fear Him;
He also will hear their cry and save them.

—Psalm 145:18-19

Remember This:

Since Jesus could bear your sins more easily than he could the thought of your helplessness, He chose to die for you.

—Max Lucado

A GIFT CARD

Giving gift cards instead of a gift for a birthday or other holiday has become a popular trend in recent years. People enjoy getting them because they can choose whatever they want from the store.

Gift cards often come with expiration dates. Sometimes I will stuff one in my wallet and forget about it. A gift card can be worth $100 one day, and then the next day you might as well throw it in the garbage because it's expired. You've missed the opportunity to spend it!

God's gift of forgiveness is like a gift card that's more valuable than anything we can imagine. He paid for it with His Son's life. God is holding that priceless gift card out to us, waiting for us to take it. However, if we don't accept it and use it, then it's of no value to us.

A gift card is only plastic unless it is redeemed. Don't wait until it's too late.

The Bible Says:

> *For the wages of sin is death, but the gift of God is eternal life in Christ Jesus our Lord.*
>
> —Romans 6:23

Remember This:

> *These days come and go, but they say nothing, and if we do not use the gifts they bring, they carry them as silently away.*
>
> —Ralph Waldo Emerson

FREQUENT FLYER MILES

My wife and I wanted to go to Hawaii and I was really close to having enough frequent flyer miles for a free ticket. Crystal had more than enough miles, so I called the airline and asked if we could use some of her "miles" for my ticket.

The woman on the other end of the line replied, "I'm sorry, Mr. Silva. Miles are nontransferable. You must acquire them personally. This program does not allow you to benefit from someone else's commitment to the program."

God's gift of salvation is like that. If I could give one of my unbelieving friends some of my faith to help him believe, I would. But I can't because the rules of heaven are similar to my frequent flyer program. God doesn't allow you to benefit from someone else's faith or commitment.

It is not possible to get into heaven because your parents are Christians, or because your spouse or best friend is a believer. You must make the commitment yourself!

The Bible Says:

> *Therefore we also pray always for you that our God would count you worthy of this calling, and fulfill all the good pleasure of His goodness and the work of faith with power.*
>
> —2 Thessalonians 1:11

Remember This:

> *There is nothing the Lord wants of us more than the exercise of our faith. He will do nothing to undermine it, and we cannot please Him without it.*
>
> —James Dobson

FALLING INTO A LAKE

Small children seem prone to falling into pools, rivers, and lakes. I will never forget the day I was at Hume Lake speaking to some students. My friend Eric's little boy was sitting in his chair right next to his daddy on the edge of the dock. All of a sudden the chair tipped over and Eric's son disappeared into the lake.

Stunned, we all watched as Eric rushed over, reached into the water, and pulled his son to safety. He did what any loving father would have done in that circumstance. In fact, Eric would have done whatever it took to save his son!

In a similar way, our loving Heavenly Father has rescued us from a certain death. The Bible says that all of us have sinned (fallen off the chair of perfection) and come short of God's desire for us. Spiritually, all of us were drowning in our sins. We were in over our heads, and God reached down and rescued us. He sent Jesus to "save" us, to pull us to safety—and to eternal life!

The Bible Says:

> *Keep my soul, and deliver me;*
> *Let me not be ashamed, for I put my trust in You.*
> —Psalm 25:20

Remember This:

> *God sits effulgent in heaven; not for a favored few,*
> *but for the universe of life, and there is no creature so*
> *poor, or so low, that he may not look up with childlike*
> *confidence, and say, "My Father, Thou art mine."*
> —Henry Ward Beecher

A TRAP

We all face traps in our personal lives. There are financial traps, moral traps, marital traps, and physical traps to name a few.

As humans, we can also create our own traps. Every summer, I set a trap out for the yellow jackets around my house. I put the bait in, and as soon as they smell it, they fly right in. My purpose is to destroy my enemy, before the nasty little guys sting me!

Satan, our enemy, is seeking to destroy us. He sets traps in our lives to turn us away from God and separate us from love and forgiveness, ultimately taking life away from us.

To avoid these traps, we must first realize that they are there! They do exist, and they can be dangerous. Also, understand that you have a choice. You can choose life instead of death, joy instead of anger, and turn to God for salvation instead of falling into the trap of the devil.

The Bible Says:

For God did not appoint us to wrath,
but to obtain salvation through our Lord Jesus Christ.
—1 Thessalonians 5:9

Remember This:

Don't try to deal with sin, for you are sure to lose.
Deal with Christ; let him deal with your sin and you are sure to win.
—Arthur Elfstrand

HEART SURGERY

A friend told me recently that his minister had just gone through open-heart surgery. Two of his three main arteries were 90 percent blocked.

When the man learned that he needed to have this surgery, he was very surprised. He said, "On the outside, I looked perfectly healthy. I hadn't noticed any problems." He appeared fine on the outside, but on the inside, he had a serious problem.

Spiritually, our problem is on the inside as well. We're self-destructing from a spiritual sickness called sin.

That's why Jesus Christ, God's Son, died on the cross to pay for our sins. We need to have open-heart surgery from the great Physician to take care of the sin problem in our lives. Then He will fill our hearts with joy and the hope of eternal life!

The Bible Says:

For Christ also suffered once for sins, the just for the unjust, that He might bring us to God, being put to death in the flesh but made alive by the Spirit.

—1 Peter 3:18

Remember This:

When you come to Christ, the Holy Spirit takes up residence in your heart. Something new is added to your life supernaturally. You are transformed by the renewing of your mind. A new power, a new dimension, a new ability to love, a new joy, a new peace—the Holy Spirit comes in and lives the Christian life through you.

—Billy Graham

$20 BILL

Have you ever felt dirty, broken, or worthless to God? I know I have been there.

If I offered you a $20 bill, would you take it? What if I wadded it up and threw it on the ground. Would you still want it? What if I stepped on it, kicked it, and even spit on it? Could I still go to the store and spend it?

The answer is yes. That bill has value because of what it is, not how it looks, where it's been, or what it's been used for. A crisp, clean $20 bill is worth the same amount as an ugly, older, more used one.

You may feel like you've been stepped on, beat up, or kicked around. You may feel dirty, unworthy or useless. But, be encouraged by the $20 bill—no matter what you've been through, you still have value to God!

The Bible Says:

Not that I have already attained, or am already perfected; but I press on, that I may lay hold of that for which Christ Jesus has also laid hold of me. Brethren, I do not count myself to have apprehended; but one thing I do, forgetting those things which are behind and reaching forward to those things which are ahead, I press toward the goal for the prize of the upward call of God in Christ Jesus.

—Philippians 3:12-14

Remember This:

Are you at the brink of despair, thinking that you cannot bear another day of heartache? Your Savior knows your breaking point. The bruising and crushing and melting process is designed to reshape you, not ruin you.
Your value is increasing the longer He lingers over you.

—Charles Swindoll

PEEKING AT PRESENTS

When I was little, I loved to sneak out to the family room at Christmastime and try to steal a peek at my presents (Actually, it was my older sister's idea!). Even as an adult, I sometimes reach over and give one a shake or try to guess what it is by how heavy it feels.

We all have a curiosity and desire to know things that are hidden. Many non-Christians have taken a peek at their Christians friends and wondered what makes them so committed to this person, Jesus Christ.

The next time you feel the need to peek at one of your presents, remember that there are many people "peeking" at Christianity who may be ready to unwrap the marvelous package of God's gift of salvation. Please be ready and willing to show them God's offer—His merciful gift of salvation!

The Bible Says:

> *But sanctify the Lord God in your hearts, and always be ready to give a defense to everyone who asks you a reason for the hope that is in you, with meekness and fear.*
>
> —1 Peter 3:15

Remember This:

> *If we made God a little more real than otherwise he would be to any single human being, we have not wasted our little lives in a large world or lived in vain.*
>
> —William Sperry

AN ESCAPE ROUTE

When you stay at a hotel, there is always a map on the wall in your room that shows the layout of the building and the exits in case of fire. Hotels have to provide an escape route.

God has provided a way for us to escape from the burning fire of hell. The Bible tells us that the way is Jesus Christ. He didn't come to condemn the world, but to save the world and redeem us.

If you don't know the way out, the fire will quickly overwhelm you. Don't wait until it's too late!

The Bible Says:

And on some have compassion, making a distinction; but others save with fear, pulling them out of the fire, hating even the garment defiled by the flesh.

—Jude 22-23

Remember This:

You are redeemed from the penalty of your sin, and you are on your way to heaven, in order that Jesus Christ might come in the power of his resurrection to occupy your redeemed humanity upon earth today, and that you might present your body a living sacrifice, totally, wholly available to him.

—Ian Thomas

HEEDING ROAD SIGNS

I love the road signs in Britain. In the United States, diamond-shaped yellow signs say, "Yield." In Britain the same signs say, "Give Way." That's exactly what the word "yield" means. We may choose to continually disobey such signs and proceed without looking, but one thing is certain—serious damage! The question is not *if*, it's simply *when*.

In the same way, God says, "I'm not trying to collide with you. I'm not trying to box you in. I simply want you to 'give way' to me so that I can protect you and allow you to be everything you were created to be."

God is saying to us, "Look at me. I am asking you to give way. Yield yourself to Jesus Christ. Trust in Him. Allow Him to pass in front of you—then draft in tight behind him. Let Him run interference for you." It's smart living! Why? Because Jesus cares more about where you are and where you are going than where you've been.

Another American road sign says, "Exit." In Britain it says, "Way Out." Whether you are at Heathrow Airport or at the underground tube, it is one thing to get in, it's quite another to get out!

My wife and I took the Piccadilly line to Piccadilly Circus. It was underground, and as we walked around in circles of wall-to-wall people, before I knew it I was lost! I felt trapped. Being lost is a miserable feeling.

Spiritually, maybe you feel lost. You feel trapped in your circumstances. You feel as if the light at the end of the tunnel is growing dim. When that happens, simply look for the sign.

Jesus Christ's mission in life is to provide a "way out" for you and for me, which explains His death on a Roman cross nearly 2,000 years ago. Why did He do it? To provide a way out! Otherwise, you and I would be trapped, lost in our sin forever. We would be wandering spiritually, confused about the future, and afraid to stop and ask for directions.

Jesus Christ is our "way out." He is the thing you have been missing but haven't known what it was or how to find it. If you say "yes" to Jesus, you are saying, "I see the sign. I want a way out. I put my faith and trust in You and You alone."

Jesus Christ is the way out of our sin, shame, guilt, and burden of wrongdoing.

The Bible Says:

That I may gain Christ and be found in Him, not having my own righteousness, which is from the law, but that which is through faith in Christ, the righteousness which is from God by faith.

—Philippians 3:8c-9

Remember This:

There are two kinds of people: those who say to God, "Thy will be done," and those to whom God says, "All right, then, have it your way."

—C. S. Lewis

NATURAL DISASTER PREPARATION

Some people will go to great lengths to prepare for an emergency or natural disaster. They not only have a flashlight, batteries, and food set aside, but some even build underground bunkers and have complicated maps which include detailed plans.

I stayed at a hotel in Korea one time that had extensively prepared for a natural disaster. In my room there was a blue vinyl bag that had a rock climbing harness in it. There were directions on how to use it and what to do in case of earthquake, power failure, natural catastrophe, etc.

When you trust Jesus Christ, the Solid Rock, you don't need to worry about how to escape the disasters of life. The Lord protects and keeps us, and will bring you safely into His eternal heaven!

The Bible Says:

> For "whoever calls on the name of the LORD shall be saved."
>
> —Romans 10:13

Remember This:

> I try not to worry about life too much because I read the last page of the book and it all turns out all right.
>
> —Billy Graham

DUTY FREE

I enjoy flipping through the "duty free" magazines available in the seat pocket of every international flight. The beauty of "duty free" is convenience and *no tax!* No matter what country you're from or what currency you use, on the airplane, you pay zero tax or fees on any item you choose to purchase.

The Bible teaches that God's gift of salvation works the same way. No one pays tax. In fact, no one pays for the product. No one jumps through a certain set of hoops to obtain God's mercy gift of salvation. Club Heaven memberships are not for sale or trade, and cannot be bought off eBay®.

If you're in the market for the unconditional love of God, total and complete forgiveness of sin, elimination of all sin, guilt, shame and wrong doing, look no further than a seat pocket in front of you! It's available for all who desire it and the best part is—it's totally *duty free!*

The Bible Says:

Not by works of righteousness which we have done, but according to His mercy He saved us, through the washing of regeneration and renewing of the Holy Spirit.

—Titus 3:5

Remember This:

Faith is to believe what you do not yet see, the reward for this faith is to see what you believe.

—Augustine

LAST MINUTE AIRLINE TICKET

Business required me to fly from Portland, Oregon, to Atlanta, Georgia. Sounds simple, right? Wrong! My office had mistakenly failed to purchase my airline ticket ahead of time.

If you buy an airline ticket a month in advance, you get a reasonable price, and if you buy it two weeks in advance, you still get an okay deal. But if you wait, you pay $1,700! You can normally fly to Australia for that princely sum.

Meanwhile, I arrived at the airport well ahead of time and checked in. You can imagine my frustration when the man behind the counter told me that he didn't have a seat for me. The flight was overbooked, and I was on the standby list.

That day I learned the difference between having a ticket and having a seat assignment! My ticketed flight took off and I stood inside the "D" Concourse watching it leave me!

In our spiritual lives, many people think that if they do enough good things on earth, they will have paid enough to earn a ticket to heaven. Not true. If you don't have a confirmed seat assignment provided only through faith alone in Jesus Christ alone, you will miss that "heavenly flight."

The Bible Says:

He who has the Son has life; he who does not have the Son of God does not have life.

—1 John 5:12

Remember This:

Faith is knowing that God is who He says He is, has what He says He has and will do what He says He will do and then putting ourselves in a position where our lives depend on it.

—Graham Steele

THROWING A TENNIS BALL

Remember what happens when you throw a ball hard against a brick or concrete wall from just a few feet away? The ball comes right back and slams you in the face!

The Bible calls this the old-fashioned "you reap what you sow" principle! And this principle is true for every facet of life. We've all "sown" mistakes, bad decisions, wrong choices, destructive habits, and painful relationships. We deserve a spiritual ball in the face.

Fortunately for us, however, God has chosen to spare us from the punishment we deserve. In fact, He has given us what we don't deserve (that's God's grace). God sent His one and only Son to pay for my sin and yours with His life and blood.

While I was throwing the spiritual dodge ball as hard as I could against the wall of life, deserving the slam in the face and complimentary bloody nose—that's when Jesus Christ stepped in front of me to block the blow of sin and death.

The Bible Says:

But God demonstrates His own love toward us,
in that while we were still sinners, Christ died for us.

—Romans 5:8

Remember This:

Lord, make me an instrument of Your peace.
Where there is hatred let me sow love;
where there is injury, pardon;
where there is despair, hope;
where there is darkness, light;
and where there is sadness, joy.

—Saint Francis of Assisi

A SEED

When you plant a seed, you don't expect it to take care of itself. The only responsibility of a seed is to be a seed. The caretaker is in charge of watering, fertilizing, and ensuring plenty of sunlight.

When it comes to salvation, we just have to be receptive. God will take care of the rest. He causes the change under the surface. He provides the essentials and the nutrients to help us along the way.

Don't try to take on more than you need to—just be the seed. There is spiritual life within you. Let God water you; let God expose you to the sunlight. Let God provide the nutrients of the soil around you. You just need to sprout! God will do His part if you allow yourself to do yours, and be receptive and ready.

The Bible Says:

> *But the [seeds] that fell on the good ground are those who, having heard the word with a noble and good heart, keep it and bear fruit with patience.*

> —Luke 8:15

Remember This:

> *Trust God for great things; with your five loaves and two fishes, he will show you a way to feed thousands.*
> —Horace Bushnell

THE WORLD'S BEST-SELLER

Avid readers are always on the lookout for the latest best seller. Every week there may be a different title at the top of the *New York Times* bestseller list, but none of them has ever sold more copies, or been printed and translated into more languages, than God's Word, the Bible.

The Bible is truly the #1 best-seller of all time. It's true year after year, decade after decade, century after century.

Did you know that the Bible is the oldest book in the world whose author is still alive? A mentor of mine says, "I know the Bible is God's Word because it finds me wherever I am." That statement cannot be said of any other book, piece of literature, or music.

The next time someone asks you what you've been reading lately, mention that you're in the middle of the world's all-time best-seller. Maybe they'll want to see what all the excitement is about!

The Bible Says:

> *For the word of God is living and powerful, and sharper than any two-edged sword, piercing even to the division of soul and spirit, and of joints and marrow, and is a discerner of the thoughts and intents of the heart.*
>
> —Hebrews 4:12

Remember This:

> *Isn't is amazing that almost everyone has an opinion to offer about the Bible, and yet so few have studied it?*
>
> —R. C. Sproul

A "V1" COMMITMENT

If you were inside the cockpit just as an airplane took off from the runway, you would hear the copilot or captain call out, "V1." This phrase represents the "point of no return."

As the airplane accelerates toward the end of the runway, the pilot must decide if it is moving fast enough for a safe takeoff. This speed must be determined preflight, because of several factors, including the air pressure, temperature, speed of the wind, and the weight of the aircraft.

The pilot maintains a hold on the throttle as V1 speed is reached, so that he or she can pull it to idle and abort the takeoff if something goes wrong. However, after V1, the plane *must* take off.

Christians should have a similar V1 commitment in our walk with Christ. Once we have placed our faith in Christ alone, we are at the go/no-go, the point of no return. We need to adjust our "attitude," apply full throttle, and take off.

When we make that V1 commitment, God will reward us by allowing us to soar to places we never dreamed of through the power of the Holy Spirit.

The Bible Says:

> *If anyone desires to come after Me, let him*
> *deny himself, and take up his cross, and follow Me.*
>
> —Matthew 16:24

Remember This:

> *All our natural powers can be used mightily by God,*
> *but only when we think nothing of them and surrender*
> *ourselves to be simply the vehicles of divine power, let-*
> *ting God use us as He wills, content to be even despised*
> *by men if He be glorified.*
>
> —G. H. Knight

SALT, PEPPER, AND KETCHUP

The other day I was putting salt and pepper on my hamburger and ketchup on my fries. As I looked at the shakers and bottle, I thought of a great analogy. Just like the wordless book, these three items could be used to present the gospel message.

In the pepper shaker, the dark specks remind us of all our sins and mistakes. The pure white specks in the salt shaker represent God and his purity. The question is: how do we go from the dirty-looking pepper to the clean salt?

The answer is the shed blood of Jesus Christ. This is where the ketchup comes in. When Jesus died on the cross, his blood was shed so that we could be cleansed from our unrighteousness.

The ketchup bottle represents the only answer for changing who we are and what we want to be.

So the next time you go for a hamburger and fries with a friend, and you see those items on your table, take the opportunity to explain this wonderful reminder of God's unconditional love for us.

Please pass the salt!

The Bible Says:

> *"Come now, and let us reason together," says the* LORD,
> *"Though your sins are like scarlet,*
> *They shall be as white as snow;*
> *Though they are red like crimson,*
> *They shall be as wool."*

—Isaiah 1:18

Remember This:

> *There is simply no way to comprehend the full implications of the love the King of Kings and Lord of Lords has for us.*

—James Dobson

A TORN CLOTH

When I see a piece of cloth torn in two, I think of the crucifixion of Jesus Christ. The Bible tells us that at that time, the veil in the Jewish Temple split in two. This veil blocked off, or separated, the Holy of Holies, where only the priests could go. Only priests could mediate between the people and God.

Now, because of Jesus Christ's death, *anyone* can come into the presence of God. We don't need a veil to block our view, or a priest to "screen" our calls for help. Because of His sacrifice, Jesus made it possible for all of us to gain immediate access to God. Today Jesus Christ is our High Priest, and we have direct access to Him, to heaven, and to all of the resources of God Himself.

The Bible Says:

Paul, an apostle of Jesus Christ by the will of God,
To the saints who are in Ephesus, and faithful in Christ
Jesus: Grace to you and peace from God our Father and
the Lord Jesus Christ. Blessed be the God and Father of
our Lord Jesus Christ, who has blessed us with every
spiritual blessing in the heavenly places in Christ.

—Ephesians 1:1-3

Remember This:

Nothing is so blessed as quiet, unbroken communication
with our Lord. The sense of the Lord's nearness, which
then fills our souls, is greater than any other peace, joy,
inner satisfaction, or security which we have known.

—O. Hallesby

A TRUST FALL

On one of our ministry trips to India, I couldn't sleep. All night I struggled with how to communicate to highly-devoted religious people that Jesus Christ loves, forgives, and longs for a personal relationship with each one.

The question was, "How can a person believe in a God they cannot see?" The answer—*trust*. The illustration I decided to use involved falling off the platform into the safe arms of several of our team members. For this illustration to be effective, of course, my part was to fall, and my friends' part was to catch!

Falling backwards into the arms of others is easy for some— and difficult for others. I think it all depends on who is catching you!

I promise you this: if you allow your faith, trust, and confidence to fall into the hands of Jesus Christ, God's Son, He will catch you—guaranteed! After all, one of the names of Jesus in the Hebrew language is "The Strongest Strong One!"

The Bible Says:

Though now you do not see Him, yet believing, you rejoice with joy inexpressible and full of glory, receiving the end of your faith—the salvation of your souls.

—1 Peter 1:8-9

Remember This:

On days when life is difficult and I feel overwhelmed, as I do fairly often, it helps to remember in my prayers that all God requires of me is to trust Him and be His friend. I find I can do that.

—Bruce Larson

CHECKING YOUR CAR BATTERY

My wife and I took a trip to visit some very close friends in southern Oregon. On the morning we were to drive home, I turned the key in the ignition, and nothing happened. Our truck was completely dead. The day before, there were no problems whatsoever, but now it would not start.

After several delays and frustrating trips to two different mechanics, we found the problem. Although the battery was good, the battery cables that connected to the posts of the battery had corroded. Over time the corrosion had built up underneath the connection. Without a good connection, the battery would not work.

We could have washed the vehicle, repainted it, made it look showroom ready, but the corrosion would still have been there, obstructing the electrical current from the battery to the ignition system.

Our sin and wrong choices have caused spiritual corrosion in our lives. And corrosion affects the essential connection or relationship with God. The only way to repair that connection is to eliminate the corrosion. That's why Jesus Christ died on the cross as a substitute for my sin and yours. His shed blood eliminated any and all corrosion of sin in our lives!

If you feel stuck or stranded, or powerless to get anywhere, don't panic. The cleansing power of the Savior's blood fixes the most corroded life!

The Bible Says:

But if we walk in the light as He is in the light,
we have fellowship with one another, and the blood of
Jesus Christ His Son cleanses us from all sin.

—1 John 1:7

Remember This:

Sin is inevitable but not necessary.

—Reinhold Niebuhr

SWATTING AT A BEE

Bees have an amazing ability to make people go crazy with fear. If a bee gets into a car, it can be disastrous.

A friend of mine told me about a little boy and his father who were driving in their truck when a bee flew in the window. The boy began to scream and cry. His father reached over and grabbed the bee and squeezed it, then threw it out the window.

The little boy was still sobbing. When his father asked what the problem was, the little boy said, "I'm afraid the bee will come back to get me."

Smiling, the father answered confidently, "I promise the bee will not get you. Look." He opened his hand and showed it to his son, saying, "Daddy took the sting for you."

What a beautiful picture of the Father's love for mankind when Jesus Christ died on the cross to take the sting of death for us. We don't have to be afraid of anything anymore. Why? Because Jesus took the sting for you!

The Bible Says:

> *O death, where is thy sting? O grave, where is thy victory? The sting of death is sin; and the strength of sin is the law. But thanks be to God, which giveth us the victory through our Lord Jesus Christ.*
>
> —1 Corinthians 15:55-57 (KJV)

Remember This:

> *There is perhaps not a phrase in the Bible that is so full of secret truth as is "The blood of Jesus." It is the secret of His incarnation, when Jesus took on flesh and blood; the secret of His obedience unto death, when He gave His life at the cross of Calvary; the secret of His love that went beyond all understanding when He bought us with His blood; the secret of the enemy and the secret of our eternal salvation.*
>
> —Corrie ten Boom

RECEIVING A GIFT

We all like to receive gifts. When our team travels overseas, we like to bring gifts to the local government officials and VIPs of the city. At our evening crusade we often give away (if appropriate) a bike, a radio, a chicken, or a bag of rice.

To put that in American perspective, that would be similar to me offering you a new Mercedes Benz car, a Harley Davidson motorcyle, or a brand-new house.

To the people in some destitute countries where we minister, a chicken makes an incredible gift. As I hold one up, I say, "I have a gift I would like to give away—who would like it?" They all raise their hands.

I explain to them that they cannot purchase this chicken because it's not for sale; they cannot earn this chicken because it is a free gift. Then I tell them that God's gift of salvation operates in the very same way!

You cannot buy God's gift of salvation, because it's not for sale. You cannot earn God's gift by working hard or being a good person. No one would have adequate time or energy to do this. All you have to do is reach out and accept the gift that He is offering.

The Bible Says:

But as many as received Him, to them He gave the right to become children of God, to those who believe in His name.

—John 1:12

Remember This:

If God had a refrigerator, your picture would be on it. If He had a wallet, your photo would be in it. He sends you flowers every spring and a sunrise every morning. Whenever you want to talk, He'll listen. He could live anywhere in the universe, and He chose your heart.

—Joe Gatuslao

SIN BITES!

As surely as a boomerang comes back to the thrower...sin comes back to the sinner!

The Bible is clear that "you reap what you sow." If we sow unrighteousness and sin, that is what will come back to bite us.

Do you receive forgiveness when you confess your sin? Absolutely. But do the consequences go away when you confess your sin? Generally not!

One way to illustrate this principle is to take a black t-shirt and an eye dropper full of bleach. Without telling anyone that it is full of bleach, write the word "sin" on the shirt with the eye dropper. At first the shirt will not look any different. However if you wait for about ten minutes, you will see "sin" in glaring letters.

We have all sinned. We can try to hide it for a while, but eventually, it will come out, and we will have to face the consequences.

Fortunately, God has offered to take care of that sin. He will wipe it away, so that even if we have to reap the immediate consequences of our actions, we won't have to face eternal punishment for our sins.

The Bible Says:

Do not be deceived, God is not mocked;
for whatever a man sows, that he will also reap.

—Galatians 6:7

Remember This:

How easy is pen-and-paper piety! I will not say it costs nothing; but it is far cheaper to work one's head than one's heart to goodness. I can write a hundred mediations sooner than subdue the least sin in my soul.

—Thomas Fuller

DEFRAGMENTING YOUR COMPUTER

Sometimes my computer starts getting really sluggish, almost spastic. One time I got so frustrated that I called one of my technologically-minded friends and had him come over to see what he could do about it.

His solution was amazingly simple: run the disk defragmenter. It is a program already installed on your computer—you simply must engage it. All of a sudden, unnecessary files were condensed or deleted. The end result was that my computer functioned like a brand-new machine!

Some people feel like their lives are so messed up and have become so out of control that there is no way that God could clean them up. Not true! Don't believe that! God has His own defragmenter for our lives that will fix us up and put us back in order.

Our heavenly Father wants to create in us a new, cleaned up life. We just have to "click yes!"

The Bible Says:

Create in me a clean heart, O God,
and renew a steadfast spirit within me.

—Psalm 51:10

Remember This:

I think that if God forgives us we must forgive ourselves.
Otherwise it is almost like setting up ourselves as a higher tribunal than Him.

—C. S. Lewis

SAYING "I DO"

For the most part, weddings are joyous occasions. (With four daughters of my own, however, bankruptcy is possible!) I love to watch the bride and groom as they express their love for each other in front of family, friends, and the Lord God of heaven and earth.

Before repeating their vows, the couple says to each other, "I do." This phrase is short and simple, yet rich with meaning. It conveys commitment, caring, and unconditional love for the other person, no matter what happens.

God's one and only Son, Jesus Christ, is saying "I do" to you today! He promises to love you unconditionally, fully, eternally, and securely. He will forgive you completely, always remain faithful to you, and never leave you or forsake you.

When He says, "I do," He means that He will be the Provider who meets all your needs, the Counselor who will assist you in navigating the challenges of life, the Father to the fatherless, and your most faithful Friend.

Then, as an expression of His love for us, Jesus Christ gave His life blood on the cross. By doing so, He historically proved and visibly demonstrated in the most incredible way of all time that He means it when He says, "I do." I do love you, I do care more about who you are and where you're going than what you've done and where you've been.

Go ahead and ask Him, "Lord Jesus, do You really, truly love me? Even after all I have said and done? Can You forgive me? Do I qualify for Your mercy gift of salvation? Are You sure You want a relationship with me in spite of who I am?" To which Jesus will smile and confidently say, "I do!"

The Bible Says:

Greater love has no one than this, than to lay down one's life for his friends.

—John 15:13

Remember This:

Measure not God's love and favour by your own feeling. The sun shines as clearly in the darkest day as it does in the brightest. The difference is not in the sun, but in some clouds which hinder the manifestation of the light thereof.

—Richard Sibbes

A MESSY ROOM

Most people would be a little embarrassed to have unexpected company when their house was a mess. My family was staying at a hotel in Nigeria, West Africa. one time when I heard a knock on the door. I opened it and found a smiling Nigerian gentleman ready to clean our room.

I was so embarrassed! My family had travel bags, curling irons, and crumpled clothing sprawled across our unmade beds. Wet towels were all over the bathroom floor.

I apologized profusely, but the young man replied graciously, "No problem, sir. For this reason I have come, to put your things in order."

The Bible says this is exactly what Jesus Christ came to do for us. To put our lives in order! He doesn't demand that we first straighten up our mess. Instead, He offers to clean up for us. He wants to forgive our mistakes and disinfect our lives.

When Jesus Christ comes knocking on the door of our hearts, and looks into our messy hearts, we need not be embarrassed. Simply open the door and listen to His voice saying, "It is for this reason I have come!"

The Bible Says:

For the Son of Man has come to seek and to save that which was lost.

—Luke 19:10

Remember This:

Few souls understand what God would accomplish in them if they were to abandon themselves unreservedly to Him and if they were to allow His grace to mold them accordingly.

—Ignatius

A TRAFFIC WARNING

I received an unexpected letter in the mail the other day. It was from my local police department. The letter informed me that radar had "caught" me exceeding the speed limit by at least ten miles per hour.

It went on to say that I would not receive an official citation, but that this was a courtesy warning. That area had some trouble with speeders, so they were monitoring it closely, and they would give out tickets in the future.

In closing, the letter reminded me that a speeding ticket could cost me up to $290. Needless to say, I took that pretty seriously, and I was much more cautious the next time I drove in that area.

The Bible is full of "courtesy warnings" from God. The Bible tells us that those who reject God's gift of salvation will receive the official citation of eternal punishment.

Next time you see a "speed limit" sign, slow down and obey the warning because someone you do not yet see might be watching you!

The Bible Says:

Therefore, as the Holy Spirit says: "Today, if you will hear His voice, do not harden your hearts as in the rebellion, in the day of trial in the wilderness."

—Hebrews 3:7-8

Remember This:

Of all the words of tongue or pen,
The saddest are these:
"It might have been."

—John Greenleaf Whittier

ORGAN DONOR

In the corner of my driver's license there's a small "D" that indicates that I am an "organ donor." That means when I die, if my organs are usable, they will be donated to enable someone else to live.

It was a fairly easy decision for me to make. After I'm dead, the organs are of no use to me! Many people have chosen to be organ donors because they like knowing that they can help save the life of a person even through their own death.

God's Son, Jesus Christ, was the first voluntary organ donor! We offer our organs after we die because it doesn't affect us while we live. However, Jesus gave up His life for all of us while He lived.

When Jesus died on the cross in my place, shed His blood, was buried, and rose on the third day, it's as if He gave me a heart transplant. He exchanged my sinful, selfish, prideful heart and put in a cleansed, holy, redeemed one!

The Bible Says:

> *Likewise He also took the cup after supper, saying, "This cup is the new covenant in My blood, which is shed for you."*
>
> —Luke 22:20

Remember This:

> *Can he have followed far who has no wound nor scar?*
> —Amy Carmichael

INSPECTING AIRLINE BAGGAGE

After returning from a trip, I opened my suitcase and discovered a fluorescent green piece of paper inside with a note.

It said: "To ensure your security and the security of your fellow passengers, the Transportation Security Administration (TSA) is inspecting all checked baggage. As part of this process, some bags are opened and physically inspected. Your bag was among those selected for physical inspection."

The TSA had to do this inspection to make sure that there was nothing inside my bag that could contaminate or endanger others' lives.

What if Almighty God decided to randomly, without notice, inspect our lives, our hearts, our minds, our actions, our deeds? What would God find? Actually, none of us would pass God's holiness test or His purity inspection.

The good news is that when we accept Jesus Christ as our Savior, God doesn't punish us for the wrong things in our lives. Instead, He cleans us up and then labels us "approved." We pass divine inspection because the blood of Jesus Christ cleanses us from all sin.

The Bible Says:

Blessed be the God and Father of our Lord Jesus Christ, who has blessed us with every spiritual blessing in the heavenly places in Christ, just as He chose us in Him before the foundation of the world, that we should be holy and without blame before Him in love.

—Ephesians 1:3-4

Remember This:

Not until we have become humble and teachable, standing in awe of God's holiness and sovereignty... acknowledging our own littleness, distrusting our own thoughts, and willing to have our minds turned upside down, can divine wisdom become ours.

—J. I. Packer

BUYING A LOTTERY TICKET

Did you know that the odds of winning an $84 million jackpot can be as small as 1 in 515,403,500? That's microscopic! And yet, people will stand in line for quite a while to purchase a ticket. In fact, some spend several hundred dollars to purchase tickets when the jackpot gets that high.

All I can say to a person who buys a lottery ticket is "Good luck!" because that is all you have—luck. There is no guarantee you will win anything. There's not even a good chance you will win. A good chance is 1 out of 15 or 1 out of 100. But lottery odds are extremely more remote than that!

For the person who seeks Jesus Christ, the odds of finding Him and receiving eternal life are 1 in 1. Jesus told us that *whoever* seeks Him will find Him!

What would you rather stake your hope on? Incredible odds that you might win some big money, or the sure thing of knowing where you will spend eternity?

One option is a incredibly slim chance. The other option is guaranteed!

The Bible Says:

> *Ask, and it will be given to you;*
> *seek, and you will find;*
> *knock, and it will be opened to you.*

—Matthew 7:7

Remember This:

> *For a small reward a man will hurry away on a long journey, while for eternal life, many will hardly take a single step.*

—Thomas Kempis

AN EMPTY BOX

When I see an empty box left over from unpacking some new piece of furniture or household appliance, I often think of the way I feel about religion.

Many people are "religious." They pack around a load of rules and regulations that say you have to live a certain way and be a certain kind of person in order to please God. However, in the end, hollow religion leaves you feeling empty, like an unused box.

As a student of "religion" I have experienced and documented that religion leaves us dissatisfied, and always wanting more. Thankfully, Jesus did not come to impose a religion. He wants a *relationship*. Instead of struggling to keep a long list of dos and don'ts, trying to be good enough for heaven, we can place our trust in Jesus Christ and what He did for us on the cross.

Our Savior wants to take those burdens and that empty feeling of "religion" and give you a real, growing relationship with the Savior of the world...Jesus Christ!

The Bible Says:

> *Come to Me, all you who labor and are heavy laden, and I will give you rest. Take My yoke upon you and learn from Me, for I am gentle and lowly in heart, and you will find rest for your souls. For My yoke is easy and My burden is light.*
>
> —Matthew 11:28-30

Remember This:

> *Religion is the story of what a sinful man tries to do for a holy God; the Gospel is the story of what a holy God has done for sinful men.*
> *Religion is good views, the Gospel is good news.*
>
> —Roy Gustafson

CAN OF PAINT

Paint can sometimes be deceiving. I learned that when I repainted my shed door frame and discovered that a lot of the wood had rotted away. The "skin" of the old paint made it look like the frame was solid, but it wasn't.

I could have put on another coat of paint. I knew, however, that it would not fix the problem. Eventually the wood would totally disintegrate.

Some people think that they can whitewash their sins by maintaining a respectable outward appearance. In reality, this only makes the problem worse. Life lived in this way is so rotten that utter destruction is imminent.

The Bible tells us that we can be forgiven and cleansed from our sins. Jesus died so that we could have an abundant and productive life. A fresh coat of paint is good, but a brand-new structure is best. We become new creations when we place our trust in Jesus Christ.

The Bible Says:

> *He who covers his sins will not prosper, But whoever confesses and forsakes them will have mercy.*
>
> —Proverbs 28:13

Remember This:

> *No matter what a man's past may have been, his future is spotless.*
>
> —John Rice

A FISHING LICENSE

I have some great friends who live in Texas. When I fish with them, I'm always required to purchase an "out of state" fishing license.

On the front of the license it simply says, "Thank you for supporting Texas parks and wildlife." I have to pay for the privilege of fishing in Texas.

As I read this, I thought, if I need a license just to catch a little fish (Actually I always seem to catch more fish than my friends do!), what kind of license will I need to enter heaven?

Thankfully, Almighty God took care of that. I paid for my fishing license with money, but Jesus Christ, God's one and only Son, paid for my access to heaven with His lifeblood.

The Bible Says:

> *Behold what manner of love the Father has bestowed on us, that we should be called children of God!*
> —1 John 3:1a

Remember This:

> *When Jesus Christ shed his blood on the cross, it was not the blood of a martyr; or the blood of one man for another; it was the life of God poured out to redeem the world.*
> —Oswald Chambers

A CAGE

When our daughters were young we enjoyed taking them to the zoo. One thing you notice at the zoo is that most of the animals are in cages. They are confined to a restricted area. In fact, they are trapped!

You may be feeling the same way. Obviously, our cages do not look like an animal's cage, but they are every bit as real. We feel trapped by financial problems. Addictions of all kinds imprison us. Many of us have relationships that have crashed and burned.

Most people wish they could break out of those things in life that imprison them, but they can't, because they're trapped.

The only way we can escape those problems is if someone other than ourselves unlocks the cage and sets us free. That's what Jesus Christ did for us through His death, burial and resurrection. Jesus Christ alone sets us free and gives us abundant, joyful, peaceful, fulfilling life.

The Bible Says:

> *Therefore if the Son makes you free, you shall be free indeed.*
>
> —John 8:36

Remember This:

> *Make me a captive Lord, then I shall be truly free.*
>
> —Augustine

BASICALLY GOOD?

Many people believe that human beings are all basically good, and that as long as we don't do anything really awful, we will all get into heaven.

Think about this: if people are basically good, why do cashiers use a special pen to check the authenticity of my $20 bill? Why are there security cameras in stores? Why do police patrol our streets even though there are posted traffic signs? Why do department stores tag clothing with an "alarm" that will sound if clothing is taken past the monitor? Why is the security screening at airports so annoying? Why do I pay to have a home security system at my house? Why is insurance fraud a multi-million-dollar-a-year racket in this country?

If evolution's theory were true, human beings should be getting better and better. So why is the prison system in the United States bursting at the seams?

The answer is that we are not basically *good*. Our tendency is to sin, lie, cheat, steal, and kill. The Bible says that every single person on the planet comes up short of God's standard. There is only one way to fix the problem of sin, selfishness, and disobedience in our lives and that is to appropriate Jesus Christ's mercy gift of salvation to our lives.

Basically good? I think not. Ask any divorce court judge! God alone is good. He has made a way for us to become forgiven, clean, and born again.

The Bible Says:

> For the law of the Spirit of life in Christ Jesus has made me free from the law of sin and death.

—Romans 8:2

Remember This:

> Going to church doesn't make you a Christian
> any more than going to the garage makes you a car.

—Laurence J. Peter

FEELING THE WIND

People ask me, "Can you prove that there is a God?"

My response is, "Absolutely, beyond a shadow of a doubt." And then I like to ask the skeptics, "Can you prove there is not?"

Think about wind. You can't see it, but you know it's real because you see or feel its *effects*. Leaves rustling in the breeze or a cold Chicago winter blast against your face.

So it is with God. The "effects" of God are visible not only at this present moment but throughout history. God always leaves His mark on the lives of the people who seek Him.

So ask me again, "Can you prove to me that there is a God?"

"Well, that depends," I'd say. "Can you prove wind exists, that gravity is true, and that the earth is rotating around the sun?"

"Absolutely," you would say, "because...." There's your answer to life's greatest question!

The Bible Says:

> *For since the creation of the world His invisible attributes are clearly seen, being understood by the things that are made, even His eternal power and Godhead, so that they are without excuse.*

—Romans 1:20

Remember This:

> *You ask me how I know he lives?*
> *He lives within my heart.*

—Alfred H. Ackley

A HELIUM BALLOON

One of the great mysteries of life is that when we die, our bodies stay on earth, but our souls leave the earth and go to heaven or hell.

To illustrate this principle to a crowd of people in West Africa, I filled several balloons with air, and others with helium. Then I let them go.

The people instantly understood that the body and spirit are two different parts. When Jesus Christ died, was buried and rose again, He enabled us to rise again also.

Just like a helium-filled balloon can rise up into the skies and disappear into the heavens, God has made a way for His followers to rise after our earthly bodies wear out and die.

The Bible Says:

Jesus said to her, "I am the resurrection and the life. He who believes in Me, though he may die, he shall live."

—John 11:25

Remember This:

"He who is born once will die twice, but he who is born twice will die once."

—E. V. Hill

OPENING A DOOR

If I came to your house and knocked on your door, and you looked out the window and saw that it was me, you would have a decision to make.

You could open the door and invite me in, or you could leave the door locked and turn away. I would be disappointed, but I would understand that I was not wanted.

Jesus uses this picture as an illustration of the way He stands at the door of our hearts and knocks. We can stay locked inside and hope He goes away, or we can open the door and invite Him in. A friend of mine says, "Jesus will never barge into a place that He is not invited to!"

It is your decision whether you will open the door and allow your life to be radically changed, or keep the door closed and ignore Christ's persistent knocking.

The Bible Says:

> *Behold, I stand at the door and knock.*
> *If anyone hears My voice and opens the door, I will*
> *come in to him and dine with him, and he with Me.*
>
> —Revelation 3:20

Remember This:

> *God hath given to man a short time here upon earth,*
> *and yet upon this short time eternity depends.*
>
> —Jeremy Taylor

PITCHING A BASEBALL

In the movie *The Rookie*, Jimmy Morris is a middle-aged man who gave up his dream of being a big league ball player because of an injury. With the encouragement of his high school baseball team, Coach Morris begins to dream again.

One night, Jimmy pulls his old truck over on the side of the roadway at one of those radar stations that indicates your speed as you drive by. Morris winds up and throws a fastball past the monitor. The number 76 is displayed briefly, and as Jimmy turns away in discouragement, he doesn't notice the 7 flicker and change to a 9. He had actually thrown the ball 96 miles per hour!

Just like Morris was completely unaware of his own ability, followers of Jesus Christ can be unaware of the power we have through the Holy Spirit. We get discouraged by our flaws and apparent weaknesses, when our Lord is simply waiting to give us the power we need!

The Bible Says:

But you shall receive power when the Holy Spirit has come upon you; and you shall be witnesses to Me in Jerusalem, and in all Judea and Samaria, and to the end of the earth.

—Acts 1:8

Remember This:

For the Christian, dependence is just another word for power.

—Bruce Wilkinson

ATTENDING A SPORTING EVENT

I love going to a baseball stadium! Not long ago I attended a San Francisco Giants' game. I handed my ticket to the attendant, and she ripped it in half and gave me the stub. As I walked into that beautiful stadium, I wondered if heaven would be anything like that. I know that heaven is not for sale. I also know that heaven is not open to the "public." It's for ticket holders only.

When God looks at you and says, "Why should I let you into my heaven? Do you have a ticket?", I pray that your answer will be, "Yes, sir, it is Jesus Christ—He alone is my ticket to heaven." Then our Heavenly Father will say, "Come on in! And enjoy the game!"

The Bible Says:

Knowing that from the Lord you will receive the reward of the inheritance; for you serve the Lord Christ.

—Colossians 3:24

Remember This:

He is no fool who gives what he cannot keep to gain what he cannot lose.

—Jim Elliot

A NEW FAMILY

I grew up in a small family. My father died when I was young, and I didn't have any brothers, but two older sisters who loved to torment me!

When I married my wife, I inherited a huge, wonderful new family. My wife is the third of seven children with aunts, uncles, and cousins like the sands of the seashore. On our wedding day, when I made a commitment to her, I also made a commitment to a brand-new family.

When you say "yes" to Jesus, you also inherit a brand new, wonderful family. No matter where you go, all over the world, there are always other Christian brothers and sisters who will treat you like family even if they've never met you before. You will have a connection and a bond that is eternal, satisfying, and enduring.

The Bible Says:

Therefore be imitators of God as dear children.
And walk in love, as Christ also has loved us and given Himself for us, an offering and a sacrifice to God for a sweet-smelling aroma.

—Ephesians 5:1-2

Remember This:

Those who live in the Lord never see each other the last time.

—German Proverb

A ROPE TRICK

The rope trick is an illusion that I like to use when I speak, and it is easy to learn. You buy a kit from a magic store that has three ropes of varying lengths. With a little slight of hand, they become equal in length!

This illustrates the fact that we all have different amounts of faith, but we can all come to Jesus just as we are. He takes our faith, whatever its quantity, and makes it more than adequate. The Bible does not say that you need a great faith; just that you need to place the faith you have in the Lord Jesus Christ.

So don't worry if your neighbor seems to have more faith than you do. What matters to God is that our faith is put in the proper place—in Him, not in ourselves, or our careers, or our money, or any other temporal "things."

The Bible Says:

But without faith it is impossible to please Him, for he who comes to God must believe that He is, and that He is a rewarder of those who diligently seek Him.

—Hebrews 11:6

Remember This:

Trust in yourself and you are doomed to disappointment; but trust in God, and you are never to be confounded in time or eternity.

—D. L. Moody

A GLOVE

When I am speaking to a group of people, I like to pull out a glove and hold it up, letting it hang loose and limp in my hand. I ask the people, "What would you like this glove to do?"

They tell the glove to do various things, like "make a fist," or "wave goodbye." Obviously, the glove does nothing.

Then I put my hand inside the glove and tell them to give the instructions over again. This time, I make the glove into a fist, wave goodbye, or blow a kiss.

The point is that the glove was not created to exist on its own. It was created to have something inside of it. Without a hand to guide it and direct it, the glove will just hang there. In the same way, you and I were not meant to exist on our own.

We each have a "God-shaped hole" in our hearts that can only be filled by Him alone. If you find yourself feeling a bit lifeless, consider that you might be missing that driving force that gives us life.

The Bible Says:

> *To them God willed to make known what are the riches of the glory of this mystery among the Gentiles: which is Christ in you, the hope of glory.*
> —Colossians 1:27

Remember This:

> *The Christian does not think God will love us because we are good, but that God will make us good because He loves us; just as the roof of a sunhouse does not attract the sun because it is bright, but becomes bright because the sun shines on it.*
> —C. S. Lewis

A FLAG

One of the things that the American flag symbolizes is freedom. It has been carried in the battles the U.S. has fought to secure that freedom, and it flies in many yards to commemorate the men and women who have died fighting for that freedom.

In India, the flag has three colors: white, red, and green. The white stands for peace, the red represents the blood shed for freedom, and the green symbolizes the fertility of the land. A wheel in the center signifies how everything works together for progress and unity.

Just as every nation's flag tells a story, I have discovered that God's story can often be found in a nation's flag. God the Father sent his Son to die so that we could live free from the power of sin and enjoy peace with God.

A flag represents the heart message of a country, and so the gospel message represents the heart of God. The next time you see a flag, discover what it means, and then see if God's message of salvation is represented there as well.

The Bible Says:

> Therefore, having been justified by faith, we have peace with God through our Lord Jesus Christ.
>
> —Romans 5:1

Remember This:

> Let a man set his heart only on doing the will of God and he is instantly free. No one can hinder him.
>
> —A. W. Tozer

A SEARCH FOR A MISSING PERSON

Many people have been found through the efforts of SAR (Search and Rescue) teams.

When a child is missing, his or her parents will not rest until the lost child is found. Love is so powerful that parents will never give up searching, hoping, believing, until the loved one is found.

Heaven works in the same way. Our loving heavenly Father never stops searching for His lost children either. We can understand a God who might forgive a sinner who comes crawling and begging for mercy, but why would Almighty God go looking for lost people like us?

The answer is that God loves us so much, and He paid such a high price for us, that He will not rest until we are found. He loves us the way a loving father loves his children—unconditionally and without end.

The Bible Says:

This is a faithful saying and worthy of all acceptance, that Christ Jesus came into the world to save sinners.

—1 Timothy 1:15

Remember This:

When you stray from His presence, He longs for you to come back. He weeps that you are missing out on His love, protection and provision. He throws His arms open, runs toward you, gathers you up, and welcomes you home.

—Charles Stanley

SUGAR

When you put sugar in your coffee or tea, do you ever think about where that sugar came from? Does sugar grow on trees? How does it become white or brown?

The truth is that sugar comes from sugar cane, which is not, in my opinion, the most attractive crop grown in the world. Sugar cane may not look like much on the outside, but its value comes from what is on the inside.

In fact, I have seen farmers overseas verify that the cane is ripe, cut off the irrigation, allow the cane stalks to dry, and then set the field on fire. Why? Because the outside of the cane is not where the value (money) is. It's what's on the inside that counts!

The same is true with us! The outside is secondary, the inside is primary. What matters is that we've had our hearts cleansed and purified from sin and shame. Having Jesus Christ on the inside is what counts. Jesus Christ refined in us makes us sweet to God!

The Bible Says:

For we are to God the fragrance of Christ among those who are being saved and among those who are perishing. To the one we are the aroma of death leading to death, and to the other the aroma of life leading to life.
—2 Corinthians 2:15-16

Remember This:

In this world of ours, that which matters most is not what happens to the outside of things, but what happens to the inside of people.

—Walter Bowie

A MICROPHONE

I have used a lot of microphones in my travels and speaking engagements, and I can tell you one thing for certain, if a microphone is not plugged in, or if the switch is not turned on, no amount of tapping or hitting it will make it work!

Microphones only work when they are connected to a power source. In the very same way, we too need a connection, a relationship with Jesus Christ in order to have spiritual power in our lives. When you are plugged in to God, you will discover that life has new significance, meaning, power, and purpose.

God wants to use your life to magnify Himself in a mighty way!

The Bible Says:

But if the Spirit of Him who raised Jesus from the dead dwells in you, He who raised Christ from the dead will also give life to your mortal bodies through His Spirit who dwells in you.

—Romans 8:11

Remember This:

Whether our work is a success or a failure has nothing to do with us. Our call is not to successful service, but to faithfulness.

—Oswald Chambers

A NEW HOUSE

My father-in-law is quietly sleeping in Room #222. After living his entire life on the farm in only two or three houses (all of which were in a five-mile radius), he's now had to move multiple times in a very short period of time. He's lived in an assisted living home, a full-time care facility, and several hospitals. Each time he has to move, it drastically changes his whole life.

When a person moves to a new place, he or she often has a change of lifestyle as well. The move gives that person a new destination, a new goal, and a new motivation.

When a person becomes a devoted follower of Jesus Christ, he or she goes through major life changes: residence, direction, destiny! We are no longer slaves to the sin nature; instead, we have a new nature that allows us to live free and fulfilled.

As Christians, we are brand-new creations. We have left our old life behind, and we have a new life in Christ, headed toward our final heavenly home.

The Bible Says:

> *Therefore, if anyone is in Christ, he is a new creation; old things have passed away; behold, all things have become new.*
>
> —2 Corinthians 5:17

Remember This:

> *It is through dying to concern for self that we are born to new life with God and others; in such dying and rebirth, we find that life is lent to be spent; and in such spending of what we are lent, we find there is an infinite supply.*
>
> —Glenn Olds

HOTEL ROOM KEY

Full-time travel is a way of life for me. Hotels are my home away from home. Several years ago I learned the trick to using those little plastic cards now called your "room key."

I insert the card at just the right speed and pull it out again, then wait for the green light to flash. When it does, you have 2.2 seconds to get that door open! The amazing part is that my key will only open my door, even though it looks the same as everyone else's key.

Guess what? We all need a key to get into God's heaven. Jesus Christ, God's one and only Son, is that programmed, designated key. It may look like a lot of other keys out there, but it is the only one that opens the door.

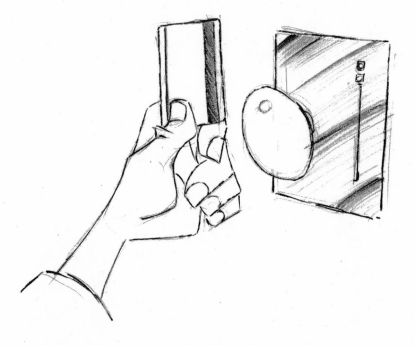

The Bible Says:

Jesus said to him, "I am the way, the truth, and the life. No one comes to the Father except through Me."

—John 14:6

Remember This:

It is not thy hold on Christ that saves thee; it is Christ. It is not thy joy in Christ that saves thee; it is Christ. It is not even thy faith in Christ, though that be the instrument; it is Christ's blood and merit.

—Charles Haddon Spurgeon

PLAYING BASKETBALL

The next time you hold a basketball, think about this interesting fact that a friend of mine pointed out to me. He said, "It all depends on whose hands it's in."

In my hands, a basketball is worth about $19.95, but that same ball in Shaquille O'Neal's hands could be worth tens of millions of dollars a year. You can say the same thing about any sport. A golf club in my hand is worth 1/10,000 of what it is worth in Tiger Woods' hands.

If you put nails in a contractor's hands, he can build a multi-million dollar house. If you put those same nails in my hands, I might be able to build an undesirable doghouse!

Now if you take those very same nails and put them in the hands of Jesus Christ, God's one and only Son, all of a sudden every sin that you have ever committed past, present, and future is eliminated. All because of whose hands it is in. That's the power of the shed blood of Jesus Christ!

My hands—you get a shabby doghouse. Jesus' hands—the forgiveness and free gift of salvation which God the Father makes available to all who place their lives into the hands of His one and only Son Jesus Christ!

The Bible Says:

Jesus said to her, "I am the resurrection and the life.
He who believes in Me, though he may die, he shall live.
And whoever lives and believes in Me shall never die.
Do you believe this?"

—John 11:25-26

Remember This:

I have held many things in my hands, and I have lost
them all, but whatever I have placed in God's hands,
that I still possess.

—Martin Luther

KNIGHT RIDERS

One of the covert branches of the military is called the "Knight Riders." Their mission and purpose? Here's a true story.

An American aviator had gone down behind enemy lines. The Knight Riders were called upon to execute the rescue. Tragically, the mission failed, and several soldiers were killed. The commanding officer briefed his team, and then said, "I need seven more men to volunteer for this mission."

The entire company stepped forward. Seven were dispatched. This time the operation was successful.

With overwhelming gratitude, the now-rescued pilot expressed his deepest appreciation. "Why did you risk your lives to come after me a second time?" the aviator asked.

The commanding officer responded, "Because our motto is: 'So that others might live!' We were doing our job."

So it is with Jesus Christ. He shed His blood, so we might live! The message of the gospel is clear. Why did Jesus die? "So that others might live!"

The Bible Says:

For God so loved the world that He gave His only begotten Son, that whoever believes in Him should not perish but have everlasting life.

For God did not send His Son into the world to condemn the world, but that the world through Him might be saved.

—John 3:16-17

Remember This:

If Christ be not risen, the dreadful consequence is not that death ends life, but that we are still in our sins.

—Geoffrey Studdert Kennedy

BURNING FLASH PAPER

If you enjoy magic tricks, you may enjoy this illustration. Purchase "flash paper" at any magic or hobby store.

Take the flash paper and write a list of sins on it. Then ask your friend, "Hey, what if I could extract from your mind every wrong, negative, selfish, lustful thought that you have ever had? What if I could extract information about every wrong relationship, every negative habit, every illegal act, and put all of those things onto a big list? How would you feel?"

Did you know every person on the planet has a sin list? The question is: how do we get rid of it? If I throw it away, someone may rummage through my garbage and find it. What if I bury it deep in the ground? With my luck, some archeologist might uncover it and publish it in the *Wall Street Journal*. There is only one solution. Eliminate the list! Completely destroy it!

The Bible says that Jesus Christ died on the cross; He became our personal sin-bearer. When Jesus died on the cross, He took my sin list and yours and—now, light the flash paper! Notice: no smoke, no ash, no residue—total and complete elimination!

All you must do is accept the forgiveness that Jesus Christ is offering you now. The work is finished; the list has been paid for. The only thing left is saying, "Thank you!"

The Bible Says:

> *Purge me with hyssop, and I shall be clean;*
> *Wash me, and I shall be whiter than snow.*

—Psalm 51:7

Remember This:

> *Heaven is full of answers to prayers*
> *for which no one ever bothered to ask.*

—Billy Graham

ROUND SPHERES

A friend of mine is a high school science teacher in Olympia, Washington. He gave me two round spheres. You can purchase your own at your local hobby or novelty shop.

Both items appear to be the exact same size, color, and weight. However, one ball bounces; the other ball does not. Why? This science teacher explained to me that the only difference between the two spheres is that one of them contains one gram of sulfur and the other does not. No sulfur—no bounce!

Sometimes people believe that a personal relationship with Jesus Christ is the same thing as attempting to be religious. Nothing could be farther from the truth. On the outside, we all may appear to be alike; however, the dynamic difference is one small ingredient on the inside.

The same is true with the identical spheres. Without the sulfur, the second ball will not bounce. In the same way, without Jesus, we cannot experience a life-changing satisfaction. Want bounce? He alone is your missing ingredient.

The Bible Says:

> *[Jesus] said to them, "But who do you say that I am?"*
> *Simon Peter answered and said,*
> *"You are the Christ, the Son of the living God."*
> —Matthew 16:15-16

Remember This:

> *The indwelling Christ, though unseen,*
> *will be made evident to others from the love*
> *which he imparts to us.*
> —Sadhu Sundar Singh

DENTAL FLOSS

Think about your last trip to the dentist. Remember sitting in the chair as the dental hygienist x-rays, scrapes, cleans and fluorides your teeth. She pulls out some floss, starts jamming it into each crack and crevice, and asks, "So, do you floss your teeth regularly?"

Now, at this point your gums are red and bleeding, so what do you say? If you say yes, she will know that you are lying, because if you were flossing regularly, your gums would not be bleeding. If you say no, you condemn yourself to a five-minute lecture on the necessity of regular brushing and flossing.

Sometimes people try to fool themselves into thinking they are right with God. They might say, "Oh, yes, I accepted Jesus when I was a child," but you can probably tell by the absence of spiritual fruit that they may not be telling you the entire truth. Just as my dentist friend says, "Your gums don't lie!"

You can't fool God either. He looks at us and sees our sore, bleeding lives, and He knows exactly what's really going on. You might be able to fool those around you, but Almighty God truly knows your heart, the validity of your relationship with Him, or the falsehood you choose to live behind.

And now you know the background of the old phrase, "You're lying through your teeth!"

The Bible Says:

> *"But every one shall die for his own iniquity:...his teeth shall be set on edge.'*
>
> —Jeremiah 31:30

Remember This:

> *Men do not differ much about what things they call evils; they differ enormously about what evils they will call excusable.*
>
> —G. K. Chesterton

A BIKE

On my last trip to India, I saw a little boy trying to sell a bicycle. At first the bike looked fine, but then I noticed that it was missing the chain. I thought, *Hmm...what good is a bike without a chain to power it?*

The frame, the wheels, the handlebars, the seat were nice, but without a chain, a bike is powerless.

You may know a person who has a good mind and a healthy body, but without a personal relationship with Jesus Christ, that person cannot truly function at maximum potential.

Investigate who God is, what He has to offer, how He can impact your life for the good. Don't just sit there: power your way through life, trusting confidently in Jesus Christ.

The Bible Says:

> *That I may know Him and the power of His resurrection, and the fellowship of His sufferings, being conformed to His death.*
>
> —Philippians 3:10

Remember This:

> *The strength of a man consists in finding out the way in which God is going, and going in that way too.*
>
> —Henry Ward Beecher

CROSSING A BRIDGE

I recently returned from El Salvador with my team. Traffic in the city we visited was almost unbelievable. When I questioned one of my Salvadorian friends as to why, he simply said "destroyed bridge."

Immediately I remembered that when God first created man, He had a perfect relationship with his creation. Unfortunately, when man chose to sin, it created a giant gulf between mankind and the holy God. Our sin demands that we be separated from the holiness of God. Sinfulness destroys the bridge of access to God.

However, God has a solution! His Son, Jesus Christ, died on the cross to pay for our sins—past, present and future. That cross has become the newly constructed bridge that allows us to travel from where we are to where we want to be.

By the time our team left the city of Soyapango, El Salvador, I had a totally different attitude about the heavy traffic and the amount of time it took to go from point A to point B.

In the beginning, I believed the problem was the traffic. Now I know the problem was the bridge. No bridge, no access!

The Bible Says:

For I am persuaded that neither death nor life,
nor angels nor principalities nor powers,
nor things present nor things to come,
nor height nor depth, nor any other created thing,
shall be able to separate us from the love of God
which is in Christ Jesus our Lord.

—Romans 8:38-39

Remember This:

If our greatest need had been information,
God would have sent an educator.
If our greatest need had been technology,
God would have sent a scientist.
If our greatest need had been money,
God would have sent an economist.
If our greatest need had been pleasure,
God would have sent an entertainer.
But our greatest need was forgiveness,
So God sent a Savior.

—Max Lucado

THE HUMAN BRAIN

The human brain has approximately twelve billion cells, with 120 trillion interconnections. The retina of an eye has over ten million photoreceptor cells that capture light and convert it into complex electrical signals to send to the brain.

Wouldn't you agree that the amazing complexity of human life is one of the great arguments for an intelligent Designer?

No one would argue that the powerful, high-speed computers we have today simply came to be after billions of years of chance. We know that men and women designed them with careful, intelligent engineering.

So why do people believe that our brains, which are much more complex than a super computer, have simply evolved over time? They try to deny it, but the truth is that the great Creator is behind all of creation!

The Bible Says:

*For You formed my inward parts; You covered me in my mother's womb. I will praise You, for I am fearfully and wonderfully made; Marvelous are Your works,
And that my soul knows very well.*

—Psalm 139:13-14

Remember This:

*All I have seen teaches me to trust
the Creator for all I have not seen.*

—Ralph Waldo Emerson

REMOVING A TUMOR

Our youngest daughter was just five years old when my wife and I had to trust a surgeon we did not know to remove a complicated lemon-sized tumor that we did not understand from our little girl's throat.

Frightened and confused, I asked the surgeon, "If this was your baby, would you do this surgery?"

Without hesitation she said, "Absolutely!" I instantly put my confidence in her. And I'm grateful to report ten years later that our daughter is a happy, healthy, miracle gift from God.

Many people have seen cancer touch the life of someone they love. It is a horrible feeling and a despised enemy. Spiritually speaking, all of us are terminally ill with a life threatening disease called sin. It's imbedded deep into our DNA. All of us need the mercy gift of life to reverse our fatal prognosis.

Only Jesus Christ, the Great Physician, can cure us. Jesus did the work on the cross when He died in your place to pay for your sin. He lives today to perform a miraculous transplant, to replace what is dead for that which is alive. He lives because He loves to forgive your sin, and give you His miraculous gift of eternal life.

The Bible Says:

Knowing this, that our old man was crucified with Him, that the body of sin might be done away with, that we should no longer be slaves of sin. For he who has died has been freed from sin.

—Romans 6:6-7

Remember This:

If you found a cure for cancer, wouldn't it be inconceivable to hide it from the rest of mankind?
How much more inconceivable to keep silent the cure from the eternal wages of death.

—Dave Davidson

FISHING

How do you handle deep-sea fishing? The last time I was out on a boat fishing, it was not a pretty sight! The sky was gray, the sea was gray, and the horizon was gray. One by one our fishing party got seasick and started dropping like flies. Just the sound of someone losing it was killing me!

I suggested that maybe we should go in. "No," the captain said, "Not as long as some are still fishing."

By noon, all of us were lying face down on the deck feeding the fish. The most wonderful words I heard all day came when the captain said, "Okay, boys and girls, since we're all in the same boat, let's go home."

In the spiritual sense, we are all in the same boat! We all suffer from the same spiritual sickness because we are all sinners; the difference is that some admit it, some don't. However, all of us come up short of God's standard.

The good news is that Jesus Christ came to forgive and cleanse us from all of our sin, sickness and unrighteousness. If you are sick and tired of being sick and tired, turn your "boat" around now and get back to the safety and stability of the harbor. You won't feel better until you do!

The Bible Says:

> *For we do not have a High Priest who cannot sympathize with our weaknesses, but was in all points tempted as we are, yet without sin. Let us therefore come boldly to the throne of grace, that we may obtain mercy and find grace to help in time of need.*
>
> —Hebrews 4:15-16

Remember This:

> *Jesus, like any good fisherman, first catches the fish; then He cleans them.*
>
> —Mark Potter

CLEANING PRODUCTS

My wife has an entire cupboard of cleaning products (in fact, two cupboards full). She tells me that we need a different substance to clean each "thing" in the house. I'm learning that cleaning products work great on what they are intended to be used for.

If only we could grab a product off the shelf to take away the stain of sin, remove the build-up of life or disinfect the mind. Unfortunately, a bottle of drain cleaner cannot fix what is wrong with the human heart.

Only the shed blood of Jesus Christ can cleanse a grungy heart like mine! Through His death, He has made us pure.

The Bible Says:

> *Surely He has borne our griefs and carried our sorrows;*
> *yet we esteemed Him stricken, smitten by God, and*
> *afflicted. But He was wounded for our transgressions,*
> *He was bruised for our iniquities; the chastisement for*
> *our peace was upon Him, and by His stripes we are*
> *healed. All we like sheep have gone astray;*
> *we have turned, every one, to his own way;*
> *and the* LORD *has laid on Him the iniquity of us all.*
>
> —Isaiah 53:4-6

Remember This:

> *Either sin is with you, lying on your shoulders, or it is*
> *lying on Christ, the Lamb of God.*
>   *Now if it is lying on your back, you are lost; but if it is*
> *resting on Christ, you are free, and you will be saved.*
> *Now choose what you want.*
>
> —Martin Luther

CLEAN AND DIRTY WATER

One of my favorite places on the planet is Hume Lake Christian Camp, in Hume, California. While speaking there at a summer camp for students one time, I used a fresh bottle of water to offer a drink to a thirsty soul and to illustrate an important point.

After a camper took a sip from the water bottle, I pulled out a little eye dropper and explained that it contained "liquid" from the sewer.

Then I added a couple of drops of the sewer water into the purified drinking water. Most often you can't even see a coloration difference, but the students knew that it was there. Most people would not want to drink the contaminated water, because the sewage has spoiled the entire bottle.

Just as a drop or two of sewer water will compromise the purity of an entire bottle of water, even the smallest drop of sin contaminates an individual's entire life!

The Bible Says:

Jesus answered and said to her, "Whoever drinks of this water will thirst again, but whoever drinks of the water that I shall give him will never thirst. But the water that I shall give him will become in him a fountain of water springing up into everlasting life."

—John 4:13-14

Remember This:

It is not necessary that every single member of the body should become useless and weak before death occurs. A weakness of, or a blow upon, the heart or the brain will suffice to bring an end to life, however strong and healthy other parts of the body may be. Thus one sin by its poisonous effect on the mind and heart is sufficient to ruin the spiritual life not of one only, but of a whole family or nation, even of the whole race.

—Sadhu Sundar Singh

A GPS DEVICE

I remember the first time I rented a car that came with a Global Positioning System (GPS) device with dozens of buttons and lights to help me navigate.

Theoretically, all you must do is enter the appropriate data—the city, street, and address of the place you desire to go, and the computer will calculate the distance and the fastest way to arrive at your destination. As you drive, a computerized voice prompts you when to turn and where to go as it guides you to your destination.

When we follow Jesus, the Bible is God's GPS for us. The Bible calculates where each turn will take us. The joy of a biblical navigation system is that using it eliminates fear of living lost!

But what if you make a wrong turn? No problem. God's navigation system simply informs you in a calm, reassuring voice, that it's "recalculating your route." It doesn't say, "Get out and let me drive," or, "Can't you follow directions, stupid?"

God's Word will always get you back on track and guide you to your ultimate desired destination. No fear, no condemnation—you're never lost with a personal relationship with Jesus Christ.

The Bible Says:

What man of you, having a hundred sheep, if he loses one of them, does not leave the ninety-nine in the wilderness, and go after the one which is lost until he finds it? And when he has found it, he lays it on his shoulders, rejoicing.

—Luke 15:4-5

Remember This:

Throughout the Bible, when God asked a man to do something, methods, means, materials and specific directions were always provided. The man had one thing to do: obey.

—Elisabeth Elliot

A WEDDING RING

Twenty-seven years ago, my wife and I gave each other wedding rings as symbols of our love, commitment, and covenant with one another. As we stood at the altar, the pastor asked, "Will you take this ring as a reminder of your lifetime commitment to your bride?"

At that moment I had a decision to make. My bride-to-be was offering me a ring, but it wasn't mine until I accepted it. I saw the ring. I knew the purpose of it. But it was not mine until I embraced it as my own.

The same is true in our commitment to Jesus Christ, God's Son. You may know that Christ died on the cross, shedding His blood to pay for your sins. You may even realize that God is offering you His gracious gift of salvation, but until you accept it personally, you do not have eternal life. There's a difference between knowing about a gift and possessing it as your own.

I have often asked men "Are you married?" As of yet, no one has responded to me with, "I think so," or "I hope so." If you're married (and don't want to sleep on the couch), you had better *know* that you are married, and specifically, to whom!

If you are really an authentic follower of Jesus, you will know it!

The Bible Says:

Salvation belongs to the LORD.
Your blessing is upon Your people.

—Psalm 3:8

Remember This:

The Christian life could be described as getting to know God better every day. A friendship which does not grow closer with the years tends to vanish with the years. And it is so with us and God.

—William Barclay

KEYS

Some people have massive key rings so large that they don't even fit into their pockets. I like to keep just two keys on my key ring—one for my house and one for my car. That way I always know if I am missing one!

There is one key that we can't afford to be without. It is the key to heaven—Jesus Christ. None of the keys we have will open heaven's door. Only trusting Him and accepting His gift of salvation will give us the key to heaven and to eternal life.

Check your key ring—nobody likes being locked out!

The Bible Says:

I [Jesus] am the door.
If anyone enters by Me, he will be saved,
and will go in and out and find pasture.

—John 10:9

Remember This:

Upon a life I did not live, upon a death I did not die;
another's life, another's death, I stake my whole eternity.

—Horatius Bonar

A POWER TOOL

Do you prefer manual tools or power tools? If you were going to build yourself a log cabin in the high country next to a spectacular fly fishing stream and you only had one week to build it, what would you reach for?

I think men will always go for the power tools—more power, *ar-ar-argh!* When it comes to a big project like that, we need energy greater than our own.

God is a Christian's power tool! There are many things in life that we can't overcome on our own strength, but He provides the extra energy and multiplies our efforts.

The Bible Says:

> *For I know the thoughts that I think toward you,*
> *says the LORD,*
> *thoughts of peace and not of evil,*
> *to give you a future and a hope.*

—Jeremiah 29:11

Remember This:

Prayer is a powerful thing, for God has bound and tied himself thereto.
None can believe how powerful prayer is, and what it is able to effect,
but those who have learned it by experience.

—Martin Luther

SECURITY SEARCH

On my way to Nicaragua, my briefcase was inspected by airport security guards. They took a little white cloth and rubbed it on the handles and all over my briefcase, searching for residue and scanning for explosives or narcotics.

My briefcase came up clean, and I was allowed to continue with my flight, but it made me wonder: how would I feel if God gave me the "white cloth test?"

If you and I were to sit before Almighty God, and if He were to take a little white cloth and rub it across my mouth and yours, across our minds and our hands and our feet, the sensors would beep so loudly that neither one of us would get into heaven.

We all have the residue of sin in our lives, and it is only the shed blood of Jesus Christ that cleanses us from all of that mess.

The Bible Says:

> *Who can say, "I have made my heart clean,*
> *I am pure from my sin"?*
>
> —Proverbs 20:9

Remember This:

> *One great power of sin is that it blinds men so that they*
> *do not recognize its true character.*
>
> —Andrew Murray

A LIGHTER

If you took a lighter and flicked the switch and placed the flame underneath a piece of paper, it would immediately begin to burn. If you put the burning piece of paper under a pile of dry kindling, you would soon have a roaring fire. From a tiny flame to a roaring fire—that's power!

Do you ever wish you had more power in your life?

Christians have a wonderful source of power—the Holy Spirit. It is not found in muscle, but in confidence, boldness, and courage. The power of the Holy Spirit comes upon every believer at the moment of salvation.

From a tiny flame, this power quickly grows into a roaring fire and empowers every Christian to do great things for God.

The Bible Says:

I [John the Baptist] indeed baptize you with water unto repentance, but He who is coming after me is mightier than I, whose sandals I am not worthy to carry.
He will baptize you with the Holy Spirit and fire.
—Matthew 3:11

Remember This:

When God is about to do something great,
he starts with a difficulty. When he is about to do something truly magnificent, he starts with an impossibility.
—Armin Gesswein

LIFE PRESERVER

Every year people drown in the frigid waters off the Oregon Coast. Sometimes people get caught by an unexpected wave or loose their footing in the powerful current.

One of the saddest circumstances occurs when someone is out on a boat without a life jacket. If the sea gets a little restless, they can quickly be swept overboard. Many people have drowned this way, and it could have been so easily prevented if they had been wearing that life preserver.

If you were drowning, and someone had a life preserver and they threw it to you, then wouldn't you jump at it and hang on for dear life?

When Jesus Christ was crucified on the cross, He died to rescue us from drowning in our sins. He is offering a life preserver to each person—wouldn't it be foolish not to take it?

The Bible Says:

> *And Jesus came and spoke to them, saying,*
> *"All authority has been given to Me in heaven and on earth. Go therefore and make disciples of all the nations, baptizing them in the name of the Father and of the Son and of the Holy Spirit, teaching them to observe all things that I have commanded you; and lo, I am with you always, even to the end of the age."*
>
> —Matthew 28:18-20

Remember This:

> *This is the mystery of the riches of divine grace for sinners; for by a wonderful exchange our sins are now not ours but Christ's, and Christ's righteousness is not Christ's but ours.*
>
> —Martin Luther

A LAMB

In ancient Bible times, the only way that sin could be forgiven was through the shedding of the blood of a spotless, perfect lamb. God accepted the lamb's blood as payment for the people's sins.

When Jesus Christ came to earth, He became the perfect Lamb that could pay for the sins of the whole world.

When I see a lamb, I remember the sacrifice that my Lord, made so that I could live. He was an innocent, pure Lamb, and He allowed Himself to be killed so that I would not have to pay the price for my sins.

The Bible Says:

The next day John saw Jesus coming toward him, and said, "Behold! The Lamb of God who takes away the sin of the world!"

—John 1:29

Remember This:

When Jesus died on the cross, He was giving "all He had" to pay the price for all the wrong things you've ever done. In your heart, for just a moment, would you walk up that hill the Bible calls Skull Hill and stand quietly at the foot of that cross where the Son of God is pouring out His life for you? Look at Him dying for you! You are not worthless! But you'll never know how valuable you are until you give yourself to the One who died to buy you back.

—Ron Hutchcraft

BRAVEHEART MOVIE

Mel Gibson's *Braveheart* is a powerful movie that portrays the sacrifice and determination of the men of Scotland in their fight for freedom from England. The main character, William Wallace, is willing to die for freedom and for his country.

That movie reminds me of how Jesus Christ was willing to die for our spiritual freedom. He didn't have to go to the cross, just like Wallace could have turned around and gone home instead of going into battle.

However, Jesus loved the world so much that He was willing to die to secure our freedom from the bondage of sin.

The Bible Says:

But, beloved, we are confident of better things concerning you, yes, things that accompany salvation, though we speak in this manner. For God is not unjust to forget your work and labor of love which you have shown toward His name, in that you have ministered to the saints, and do minister. And we desire that each one of you show the same diligence to the full assurance of hope until the end, that you do not become sluggish, but imitate those who through faith and patience inherit the promises.

—Hebrews 6:9-12

Remember This:

That God is more near, more real and mighty, more full of love, and more ready to help every one of us than any one of us realizes, is the undying message of the Gospels.

—David Cairns

NAILS

To vividly illustrate the concept of forgiveness, get a block of wood and some nails. Invite your friends to help you hammer the nails into the wood.

The nails represent all the sin and hurt in our lives. Pain, hopelessness, disappointment, bitterness, failure, abandonment, etc., have all kept us from experiencing the joy of God's forgiveness.

When we hammer those nails into the wood, it reminds us of how Jesus Christ allowed nails to be pounded into His hands and feet so that He could be the ultimate sacrifice for us. He took the punishment we deserved, and now we can be free.

The Bible Says:

The thief does not come except to steal, and to kill, and to destroy. I have come that they may have life, and that they may have it more abundantly.

—John 10:10

Remember This:

Forgiveness is a rebirth of hope, a reorganization of thought, and a reconstruction of dreams.
Once forgiving begins, dreams can be rebuilt.

—Beverly Flanigan

LOST COIN

In the ancient Middle East, when a young woman married, she received a headband with ten silver coins on it. This headband signified that she was married and was a symbol of status and importance. If she were to lose one of the coins from the headband, she would enlist her entire family to help her search for the missing coin.

In Jewish tradition, a man would often give a woman a coin or several coins to symbolize his promise to marry her. These coins held great value.

Jesus tells a story in Luke 15 of a woman who lost a coin. She stopped everything, lit a lamp, and searched for the coin until she found it. When she did, she called all her friends over to celebrate.

The Bible tells us that Jesus feels the same way about every person that comes to Him!

The Bible Says:

Likewise, I say to you, there is joy in the presence of the angels of God over one sinner who repents.

—Luke 15:10

Remember This:

God could, if I may say so, more easily have made a new world of innocent creatures, and have governed them by the old covenant, than have established this new one for the salvation of poor sinners; but then, where had been the glory of forgiveness?

—John Owen

A FERRY OR BARGE

The river was huge, muddy, and strong. I can still see it in my mind. Without the ferry, crossing would have been impossible. We were in Guyana, South America. The only way to our destination was that boat. There was no bridge, road, railway, foot path, or zip line. Without the ferry, we would have remained "cut off," separated from our destination.

Just as the boat was the only way to cross the river, Jesus Christ is the only way to get to God. There is no way we can make it on our own—the river is too enormous, too dangerous to navigate.

Thankfully, our loving Lord provided a way for us to cross safely. Jesus' death, burial and resurrection make it possible for us to cross over from one side of life where we are, to a new life with Him, where we want to be. There is only one way to get to heaven, and Jesus is that way!

The Bible Says:

For even the Son of Man did not come to be served,
but to serve, and to give His life a ransom for many.

—Mark 10:45

Remember This:

Perhaps only when human effort had done its best and
failed, would God's power alone be free to work.

—Corrie ten Boom

WINDSHIELD WIPERS

Matthew is a little boy in our church. His mother told me recently about a day that they were driving together in the rain. "Mom," he said, "I am thinking of something."

This announcement usually meant that he had been pondering some fact for a while and was now ready to expound on all that his seven-year-old mind had discovered. His mom replied, "What are you thinking?"

He said, "I'm thinking that the rain is like sin, and the windshield wipers are like God wiping our sins away."

"That is really good," she told him, curious at this new revelation. "Do you notice that the rain keeps coming down? What does that tell you?"

Matthew didn't hesitate one moment with his answer. "We keep on sinning and God just keeps on forgiving."

Matthew was right! God keeps on forgiving, even when we keep on sinning. The next time you are watching the rain pound down against the windshield of your car, remember that He is always faithful to forgive us.

The Bible Says:

If we confess our sins, He is faithful and just to forgive us our sins and to cleanse us from all unrighteousness.

—1 John 1:9

Remember This:

When you begin to understand just how weak, helpless, and sinful you really are, you've made a beginning.

—R. R. Ball

OPENING AN ENVELOPE

We all love to get checks and encouraging letters in the mail. When I go to my mailbox and find an unexpected note from an old friend, it always brings a smile to my face.

When God sent his Son Jesus to the earth, it was as if He were sending us a personal message just to say, "I love you."

God's message to you today is this: "I care about you, and you matter to Me. To prove it, I am going to allow My Son (Jesus) to be beaten, tortured, and executed to pay for your sins. Even before you ask, I will take care of the punishment you deserve for all of your wrongdoing—your sin, selfishness, and pride."

That message is just as valid today as it was 2,000 years ago. Our loving heavenly Father has a letter for each of us, but we have to open it and embrace the message inside!

The Bible Says:

- *Casting all your care upon Him,*
  for He cares for you.

—1 Peter 5:7

Remember This:

In the absence of the human voice, there is nothing like the written word: thoughts put down by the hand of someone you love. These are thoughts that can be touched, thoughts that can be discovered down through the years, folded and tucked like treasure inside a drawer.

—Bob Greene

INSURANCE POLICY

These days it seems one has to have insurance for almost everything. Fire insurance, earthquake insurance, flood insurance, health insurance, life insurance, homeowner's insurance, and car insurance—a person can even purchase wedding insurance in case anything goes wrong on your special day!

Jesus Christ provides a lot more than just "fire" insurance for the future. When an individual says "yes" to Jesus Christ, there are some immediate benefits every believer enjoys! For example: love, joy, peace, purpose, patience, goodness, kindness, wisdom and self-control (the power to make right choices).

Jesus Christ's insurance has incredible benefits, an eternal reward program, and (best of all) it's free to you!

No prequalification necessary. No one is ever denied coverage. None! God accepts you just the way you are. His office is always open and His phone is never unplugged. Don't worry about voicemail; the Lord personally answers every call, all the time.

The Bible Says:

Call to Me, and I will answer you, and show you great and mighty things, which you do not know.

—Jeremiah 33:3

Remember This:

Joy is the flag you fly when the Prince of Peace is in residence within your heart.

—Wilfred Peterson

POLE HOUSES

In several countries around the world, people build their homes high upon platforms to protect their families and their belongings from dangers such as floodwaters, wild animals, and thieves. Their elevation keeps them from experiencing the destruction that is going on below them.

When Jesus Christ died on the cross, canceling the debt of our sin, He elevated us from the destructive effects of sin in our lives. To protect us from the dangers that surrounded us, Jesus paid with His life.

The Bible Says:

> No one has ascended to heaven but He who came down from heaven, that is, the Son of Man who is in heaven. And as Moses lifted up the serpent in the wilderness, even so must the Son of Man be lifted up.
>
> —John 3:13-14

Remember This:

> Our hope is the Promise, not the possibilities. Although I can have hope for better health, what I need to rest in is the promise that God will sustain me in all circumstances and provide me a residence in His presence, no matter what.
>
> —Jim Arnold

A CHILD IN A MUD PUDDLE

Many children seem to have little magnets inside of them that attract them to big mud puddles.

On a trip overseas my hotel window overlooked a children's schoolyard. Watching a strong tropical rain pelt the earth, I noticed a little girl had escaped from her classroom and began to play in a puddle.

A woman came out to capture the little runaway and put her back inside where she was supposed to be. However, the little girl ran straight to the big puddle and sat down! Now two teachers came to assist but she screamed, kicked, and splashed dirty puddle water all over the visibly frustrated women.

In some ways, I am like that little girl. I too want to go my own way, to do what I want, and I don't appreciate being denied what I want! Humans are naturally prone to wander, aren't they?

Because of our disobedience, stubbornness and rebellion, Jesus had to die on the cross to pay for and counteract my sinful choices.

The Bible Says:

All we like sheep have gone astray; we have turned, every one, to his own way; and the LORD has laid on Him the iniquity of us all.

—Isaiah 53:6

Remember This:

Some people do not like to hear much of repentance; but I think it is so necessary that if I should die in the pulpit, I would desire to die preaching repentance, and if out of the pulpit I would desire to die practicing it.

—Matthew Henry

IMMIGRATING TO THE UNITED STATES

Every year, thousands of people from countries around the world attempt to immigrate to the United States. Many leave their own country for reasons of poverty, persecution, famine, terrorism, and war.

In order to come into the United States, however, there are many requirements. For example, an immigrant needs a sponsor. A citizen of the United States (spouse, family member, or friend) must agree to take care of the person until he or she finds a job. An immigrant cannot simply come into the country on his or her own merit.

Heaven operates in a similar way. None of us can get to heaven on our own. We are required to obtain a sponsor—and that sponsor is Jesus Christ! He vouches for us before the Father, and makes the provisions necessary for us to have eternal life. We are not qualified on our own merits, but God has made a way for us through His gracious Son.

The Bible Says:

Just as He chose us in Him before the foundation of the world, that we should be holy and without blame before Him in love, having predestined us to adoption as sons by Jesus Christ to Himself, according to the good pleasure of His will, to the praise of the glory of His grace, by which He made us accepted in the Beloved. In Him we have redemption through His blood, the forgiveness of sins, according to the riches of His grace.

—Ephesians 1:4-7

Remember This:

And the longer you delay, the more your sin gets strength and rooting. If you cannot bend a twig, how will you be able to bend it when it is a tree?

—Richard Baxter

THE ROCK

I want to thank my friend Larry for teaching me the rock principle! The San Francisco Bay is huge. So is the infamous Golden Gate Bridge that crosses it. Have you ever tried to pick up a rock and throw it across the bay? I have. It's not possible.

Some of you may undoubtedly be able to throw the rock farther than I can. I am sure I could throw the rock farther than some of you can. But the point is that no one can throw a rock all the way across the San Francisco Bay. All of us would come up short!

Every one of us falls short of God's standard of perfection. Who can throw farthest is of no value if the goal is to reach the other side.

We all need Jesus Christ to wash away our sins and make us holy before God. With His help, we can make it to our destination. Without Him, we will fall short!

The Bible Says:

For all have sinned and fall short of the glory of God.
—Romans 3:23

Remember This:

God is great, and therefore he will be sought; he is good and therefore he will be found.
—John Jay

LIGHTS, CAMERA, ACTION!

We have camcorders, digital cameras, and other devices now that can record almost anything. Sometimes we aren't even aware that we're being taped.

I wonder what it would be like if we could see a recording of our entire lives. Obviously God sees everything that goes on in our lives, good and bad.

How would you feel if God had a recording of everything you have ever said wrong? What if he recorded every negative attitude, harmful relationship, secret habit, and lying word?

I've got good news for you! When Jesus Christ died on the cross, in our place, and shed His blood to pay for our sin, He eliminated, or "edited out," everything that's been recorded. God forgives us completely for those sins and eliminates every trace of evidence.

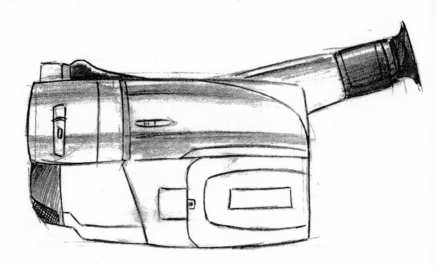

The Bible Says:

For as the heavens are high above the earth,
so great is His mercy toward those who fear Him;
as far as the east is from the west,
so far has He removed our transgressions from us.

—Psalm 103:11-12

Remember This:

There are, even today, a great many people who under-
stand that man needs salvation,
but there are very few who are convinced that he needs
forgiveness and redemption....
Sin is understood as imperfection, sensuality, worldli-
ness—but not as guilt.

—Emil Brunner

BOILING WATER

Personally, I don't believe that everyone who claims to be a Christian is one. Want proof? If you looked at a pan of water, how would you know if it was really hot? You could tell by whether or not it was boiling.

If there were no visible results of the water being hot, you would probably doubt that it was. You would need to see steam rising or feel the heat against your skin—you would want visible or tangible proof.

Likewise, if you don't see the fruit of the Holy Spirit evident in a person's life, you may want to question the validity of their claims. Because if you've got Jesus, you've got a changed life!

A relationship with Jesus changes you—and the change is visibly evident!

The Bible Says:

> *Either make the tree good and its fruit good, or else make the tree bad and its fruit bad; for a tree is known by its fruit.*

> —Matthew 12:33

Remember This:

> *If you do not worship God seven days a week, you do not worship Him on one day a week. There is no such thing known in heaven as Sunday worship unless it is accompanied by Monday worship and Tuesday worship and so on.*

> —A. W. Tozer

AN ATM CARD

I need a pin number or code for just about everything these days. When I get locked out of my house, I just go over to the lockbox and punch in a code. I need a code to access my bank account, my credit card, and even my car door!

When you get to heaven, you will need a "code" there as well. You can try your birth date, your anniversary, or your social security number, but they won't work. Only one code matters when you get to heaven—and it's not a number, it's a name!

The access code of heaven is simply "Jesus"! No other code name works.

The Bible Says:

And it shall come to pass that whoever calls on the name of the Lord shall be saved.

—Acts 2:21

Remember This:

The hope of heaven under troubles is like wind and sails to the soul.

—Samuel Rutherford

QUALIFYING

I have met people who feel as if they have messed up their lives so much that they don't qualify to be a Christian. They think that God could never forgive all the bad things they've done. I have news for those people: they are exactly the kind of people Jesus came to save!

A friend of mine in south Texas taught me this principle clearly. If your house were on fire, you would qualify for the fire department. If you are sixteen, and you pass the written exam and the driving test, you qualify for a driver's license.

If you pass four years of high school, you qualify for a diploma. If you were hurt in a car accident, you would automatically qualify for a trip to the hospital.

So the obvious question is this. How do you qualify for being a Christian? Well, if you've messed up and made some mistakes, and gone down some wrong paths, then you "qualify" for a Savior!

The Bible Says:

Jesus answered and said to them, "Those who are well have no need of a physician, but those who are sick. I have not come to call the righteous, but sinners, to repentance."

—Luke 5:31-32

Remember This:

The deepest need of men is not food and clothing and shelter, important as they are. It is God.

—Thomas R. Kelly

THE EMPEROR'S CLOTHES

Do you remember the fairy tale about the emperor who had some tailors come in to make him a new set of clothes? The tailors convinced the emperor that only the very wisest people could see the clothes, so the emperor was ashamed to admit that he saw nothing.

It took a child to finally point out that the emperor was not wearing anything. He was quite embarrassed when he realized that he had been fooled.

Sometimes we are fooled into thinking that we don't need God. We think that we have it all together and our life is pretty good. The Bible tells us that kind of thinking is foolish.

God gave us the law to point out that we can never be good enough. Then He sent Jesus to provide the solution. Even though we're not perfect, He has paid for our sins and made us holy before God!

The Bible Says:

If we say that we have no sin, we deceive ourselves, and the truth is not in us.

—1 John 1:8

Remember This:

Mere knowledge is not enough to undercut the evil in the human heart. Simply knowing what is right doesn't enable us to do right.

—Chuck Colson

ELECTRIC FENCE

My friend Sam was feeding apples to my horse. When his elbow accidentally touched the electric fence, my horse bolted from the shock. Sam realized he had touched the hot wire, but the horse took the zap!

When you touch an electric fence, the shock has to go somewhere. If not right into you, it will pass through you to whatever else you are touching, continuing to go through people or other conductors until it finds something to land on.

Sin also has a "shock." When we choose to touch sin, it has consequences. However, because Jesus Christ died and shed His blood on the cross, He took the painful shock for us!

The consequential "zap" of our sin should go to us, but instead it goes right through us, and Jesus takes the payment for all our wrong choices, selfish behavior, and bad attitudes.

The Bible Says:

> *[Jesus] Himself bore our sins in His own body on the tree,*
> *that we, having died to sins, might live for righteousness—*
> *by whose stripes you were healed.*

—1 Peter 2:24

Remember This:

> *Does God really love us?*
> *I say look to the crucified Jesus.*
> *By every drop of sinless blood that fell to the ground.*
> *By every breath of pain which Jesus drew upon the cross.*
> *By every beat of His loving heart.*
> *God said, "I love you!"*

—Billy Lobbs

A BABY

I remember when my first daughter was born. I was amazed at how tiny she was. As I held her in my arms, I realized that I had a great responsibility now. Newborn babies are completely dependent on others for everything—feeding, clothing, bathing, warmth, etc. This new little one would need me just to stay alive.

When Jesus came to earth, He didn't come as a great king, even though that's what He deserved. He came as a tiny, helpless baby, needing everything to be done for Him. Can you imagine how humbling that would be for the powerful God of the universe to become the most helpless creature on earth?

The reason He did it was to show that He came not as a Conqueror, but as a Servant, to sacrifice His life for us. He loved us so much that He became nothing so that He could give us everything.

The Bible Says:

And being found in appearance as a man,
He humbled Himself and became obedient to the point
of death, even the death of the cross.

—Philippians 2:8

Remember This:

There is nothing we can do to make God love us more,
there is nothing we can do to make God love us less.

—Philip Yancey

PREPAID PHONE CARD

Telephoning the United States from overseas can be extremely difficult. One time a friend of mine took along a prepaid phone card on an international trip so that he could use it to call home. He even called the phone company first to make sure it would work.

Well, much to his dismay, he couldn't get the card to work the entire trip. Then he read the very small print on the back. "[This company] makes no express or implied representations or warranties about its services and furthermore, disclaims any implied warranties." What does that mean? Nothing! If you can't get through, it's not their fault.

The card might work in the United States, but without the right international access code, he just had a worthless piece of plastic!

When I was young, I was very "religious." I went to church, gave money, and tried to be good. But it didn't save me or change me. I had the religious card, but I didn't have the necessary access code. You need Jesus Christ as your Savior to get through to God!

The Bible Says:

He who believes in Me, as the Scripture has said,
out of his heart will flow rivers of living water.

—John 7:38

Remember This:

The New Testament does not say,
"You shall know the rules, and by them you shall be
bound," but, "You shall know the truth, and the truth
shall make you free."

—John Baillie

SPYWARE

My friend Mike noticed that things were not quite right with his computer the other day. Advertisements began to pop up consistently every time he tried to visit a web page. So he downloaded a product designed to find and remove spyware. When he ran the program, it found thirty-five occurrences of spyware on his computer.

It said, "Your system has been compromised. Do you want to fix it?" When he clicked yes, it began the process of identifying and removing unauthorized spyware components on his system.

Sounds like us, doesn't it? Sometimes we expose ourselves to something, and we don't even know that we our compromising our system until little signs begin to pop up. The Spirit of God and the Word of God act like an anti-spyware program.

The Holy Spirit tells us when our life has been contaminated and asks, "Do you want to fix it?" When you say "yes" to God, He comes in and cleans up those parts of life that have been compromised.

The Bible Says:

> The law of the LORD is perfect, converting the soul; the testimony of the LORD is sure, making wise the simple; the statutes of the LORD are right, rejoicing the heart; the commandment of the LORD is pure, enlightening the eyes; the fear of the LORD is clean, enduring forever; the judgments of the LORD are true and righteous altogether.
>
> —Psalm 19:7-9

Remember This:

> It's bad when you fail morally.
> It's worse when you don't repent.
>
> —Luis Palau

A LAWNMOWER

Every time I come back from a trip, I find my lawn desperately needs to be mowed. It seems to grow twice as fast while I'm gone, and I always come back to find it unkempt, overgrown, and out-of-control.

I am usually too tired to get out there and mow it right away, so I end up looking at it for a few days, wishing it would go away. Eventually I resign myself to the fact that all of my wishing isn't going to make that lawn cut itself. I have to get out there with the lawnmower and put some work into it!

Mowers are designed to manicure lawns in the same way that Jesus Christ is able to manicure everything overgrown and out-of-control in our lives.

My lawn will not mow itself, and we cannot fix ourselves spiritually. We must allow Jesus Christ to take control of our lives. If you find your life is a little bit overgrown or unkempt,

simply pray this little prayer. "Lord Jesus, I'm asking You to do for me what I cannot do for myself. I want to become the person that You created me to be."

The Bible Says:

I would have lost heart, unless I had believed that I would see the goodness of the Lord in the land of the living. Wait on the Lord; be of good courage, and He shall strengthen your heart; wait, I say, on the Lord!

—Psalm 27:13-14

Remember This:

Faith is putting all your eggs in God's basket, then counting your blessings before they hatch.

—Ramona Carroll

MOSQUITOES

Our team was in India one time, talking in the lobby of our hotel, when the manager approached us. "Sirs, please be advised that we are preparing to spray for mosquitoes." We cleared out and he pulled out the spray. The little critters never saw it coming. Instantly, they began to die.

I usually announce to whoever is around my home in the summer months that I am heading out to "spray" so they can stay clear of the fumes, but unfortunately the mosquitoes don't understand my warning. If I really cared about those pests (but I don't), and I could become like one of them, then I could fly around and warn them that the spray was coming so they could escape. That would be their only hope.

Our loving heavenly Father wanted to communicate His love so much that He sent his Son to become one of us so that He could warn us of impending judgment on sin.

Compared to the great God, we are as insignificant as little mosquitoes. However, God doesn't see us that way. He sees us as His creation, and He loves us. That is why Jesus Christ died in our place—because He knew what was coming, and what we needed to survive.

The Bible Says:

> For the Son of Man has come to save that which was lost.
>
> —Matthew 18:11

Remember This:

> The saints are the sinners who keep on trying.
>
> —Robert Louis Stevenson

CALLING 9-1-1

If you were to call 9-1-1 right now, you would hear a dispatcher on the other end who would say, "This is 9-1-1, what is your emergency?" Staff people are ready to assist whenever you need help, no matter what time of day, no matter what day of the year.

One call will activate the specific assistance you need—a paramedic, fire department, or a police officer. Think about it, twenty-four hours a day, seven days a week, every week of the year! Now that's service!

Almighty God operates this very same way. Whether you are feeling lonely, afraid, or in need of instantaneous help, He is always ready to assist. In fact, contacting the Lord is faster and easier than a 9-1-1 call. And since the call is wireless and voice activated, "Lord, help!" is all that it takes to dispatch the resources of heaven!

The Bible Says:

And my God shall supply all your need according to His riches in glory by Christ Jesus.

—Philippians 4:19

Remember This:

There is nothing so strong or safe, in any emergency of life, as simple truth.

—Charles Dickens

CASHING A CHECK

If I walked into a bank that wasn't my own, and I tried to write a check to get back $3,000 in cash, the teller would look at me and say, "I'm sorry, if you don't have an account with us, I cannot give you any money." Do you know how I know this? That's right, because I've tried!

But what if my friend was the president of the bank? If he came in and said to the teller, "You can cash this check on my behalf," then I would get my money right away! The secret is in who you know.

To become a child of God, all that matters is who you know. If you know Jesus Christ, you have instant access to Almighty God.

It's not important *what* you know—you can know about the Bible and the history of the Church, and many other things—but if you don't have a personal relationship with Jesus Christ, God's Son, your "check" is worthless.

The Bible Says:

For I am not ashamed of the gospel of Christ, for it is the power of God to salvation for everyone who believes.

—Romans 1:16

Remember This:

Nothing can alter the character of God. In the course of a human life, tastes and outlook and temper may change radically; a kind, equable man may turn bitter and crotchety; a man of good-will may grow cynical and callous. But nothing of this sort happens to the Creator. He never becomes less truthful, or merciful, or just, or good, than He used to be. The character of God is today, and always will be, exactly what it was in Bible times.

—J. I. Packer

INK CARTRIDGE

The great folks with whom I work know that "technology" and computers are not my area of expertise. So when my printer ran out of ink, it was quite a chore for me to replace the cartridge.

When I finally figured out what kind of printer I had, I forgot to write down the model number, so I ending up making several trips to the store. Finally, I installed the new cartridge, closed the lid, and tried to print something. "Error – blockage" the printer told me. Nothing worked. Finally I called a friend of mine. He explained that I needed to remove the little green piece of tape from the bottom of the cartridge.

Once I pulled the tape off and reinstalled the cartridge, it worked perfectly, just as it was designed to.

Spiritually, even if you do and say all the right things and work hard, if there's something blocking your personal connection with God, you will not function as you were designed to!

The Bible Says:

Knowing that a man is not justified by the works of the law but by faith in Jesus Christ, even we have believed in Christ Jesus, that we might be justified by faith in Christ and not by the works of the law; for by the works of the law no flesh shall be justified.

—Galatians 2:16

Remember This:

If you intend to accomplish anything, if you mean not to labor in vain or spend your strength for nothing; you must take your side. There can be no halting between two opinions. You must coolly, firmly and irrevocably make your determination and resolve that the Lord is your God, and that you will serve him only.

—Timothy Dwight

AAA MEMBERSHIP

The other day I received my new AAA membership card in the mail. This card means that when my vehicle breaks down, I simply call the 800 number on the back of my card and someone shows up to help me.

Having a personal relationship with Jesus Christ is kind of like having an AAA membership. If you are a member of God's family, you have instant access to His emergency help line. Whether you break down completely or just need a flat tire repair, assistance is available and on the way!

No matter what struggles you face today, remember that Jesus loves you, and values you. He lived and died to provide peace of mind membership coverage for you and your family.

The Bible Says:

> Peace I leave with you, My peace I give to you; not as the world gives do I give to you. Let not your heart be troubled, neither let it be afraid.
>
> —John 14:27

Remember This:

> Those who go to Heaven ride on a pass and enter into blessings that they never earned, but all who go to hell pay their own way.
>
> —John R. Rice

GETTING ON AN AIRPLANE

Flying requires a lot of trust. When you step onto an airplane, you are putting your life in the hands of a complete stranger. Most of the time, none of the passengers on the plane have any idea how to fly the aircraft. Only the pilot and copilot know how to get everyone safely to their destination.

If you can trust the pilot and the equipment of an airplane with your life, how much more should you be able to trust God with your life? Pilots have been known to make mistakes, and airplane equipment has failed before.

But God has never failed! He always comes through for His people. You don't need to be afraid to trust Him with your life and your future, because He is all-powerful and He knows what you need even before you need it.

When you transfer your trust to Jesus Christ, you can be sure that He's got the equipment and the ability to get you safely to your future destination!

The Bible Says:

Let not your heart be troubled; you believe in God, believe also in Me. In My Father's house are many mansions; if it were not so, I would have told you. I go to prepare a place for you. And if I go and prepare a place for you, I will come again and receive you to Myself; that where I am, there you may be also.

—John 14:1-3

Remember This:

If God were small enough to be understood, He would not be big enough to be worshiped.

—Evelyn Underhill

EATING FRENCH FRIES

Picture your favorite fast food restaurant and imagine that you are standing in line to order. Not being overly hungry, you simply plan to order a bacon cheeseburger. Then the person behind the counter smiles and asks you "Would you like fries with that?"

"Oh, sure," you say. Now that you mention it, fries do sound good. Think about how many times you have ordered fries or super-sized your meal just because the person behind the counter "invited" you to.

In a similar way, many lost and hurting people out there are just waiting in line for an invitation. They're waiting for a gentle tug from a trusted friend! A friendly dinner out, concert, or

special event at your church may be just the thing to lift their spirits and get them interested in Christianity.

The next time you are grabbing a quick bite to eat with an unsaved friend, remember that they may really want to supersize it, but you'll never know unless you invite them!

The Bible Says:

But go and learn what this means: "I desire mercy and not sacrifice." For I did not come to call the righteous, but sinners, to repentance.

—Matthew 9:13

Remember This:

When I enter that beautiful city
And the saints all around me appear,
I hope that someone will tell me,
"It was you who invited me here!"

—*Corrie ten Boom*

A TALL TREE

The Giant Sequoia Redwood is the largest living organism in the world and is only found on the western slope of the Sierra Nevadas in California. The famous "General Sherman" is 275 feet tall and weighs an estimated 2.7 million pounds. At its base, General Sherman is 103 feet in circumference. So that one tree takes up 52,508 cubic feet of space!

Sequoia trees start out as tiny seeds. One day Jesus was walking with his followers when He bent down and picked up a little seed from the ground. He held it on His finger and said to His disciples, "If you had faith as small as this mustard tree seed, you could move mountains."

Jesus didn't say, "If you have faith as big and strong as a Giant Sequoia, you could move a mountain." Your faith doesn't have to be as great as the apostle Paul's or one of the other biblical heroes. Jesus just asks that we have faith (even a small amount). Why? Because He will grow it into giant faith!

The Bible Says:

> *If you have faith as a mustard seed, you will say to this mountain, "Move from here to there," and it will move; and nothing will be impossible for you.*
>
> —Matthew 17:20

Remember This:

> *In Christ may be seen that for which the whole universe has come into existence.*
>
> —Edwyn Bevan

TAKING PICTURES

When you snap a roll of pictures with your 35mm camera, and take the film in to be developed, you expect them to turn out. Even though you can't see the pictures, you believe that they are there in that little box.

Faith is exactly like that! You take a photo and you say, "I haven't seen it, but I know it's there." We've all taken pictures that didn't turn out the way we expected—too dark, too far away, out of focus, or maybe they got lost in the photo lab.

But faith in Jesus Christ will always be a sure thing. You can trust Him as the photo-finisher of your life. He will come out perfect on your behalf every time.

The Bible Says:

> *Looking unto Jesus, the author and finisher of our faith, who for the joy that was set before Him endured the cross, despising the shame, and has sat down at the right hand of the throne of God.*
>
> —Hebrews 12:2

Remember This:

> *The will of God will never take you to where the grace of God will not protect you. To gain that which is worth having, it may be necessary to lose everything else.*
>
> —Bernadette Devlin

GETTING LOST

My wife and I were driving through a rural area trying to reach an appointment. She kept asking me to consult the road map, but I insisted that I knew where I was going. However, it soon became clear that we were lost.

I was shocked when I discovered that we weren't just slightly off course, but we were headed in the *opposite* direction from where we needed to go. I stopped, turned the car around, and began driving according to the map. Eventually, we reached our destination.

Many times in our lives we could have avoided a long detour or an unfortunate accident if we had just consulted the map.

God has given us the Bible as a road map for life. If you find yourself feeling lost or going in the wrong direction, please stop and check it out. It's never too late to turn around and go in the right direction.

The Bible Says:

All Scripture is given by inspiration of God, and is profitable for doctrine, for reproof, for correction, for instruction in righteousness, that the man of God may be complete, thoroughly equipped for every good work.
—2 Timothy 3:16-17

Remember This:

Only he who can say, "The Lord is the strength of my life" can say, "Of whom shall I be afraid?"
—Alexander MacLaren

Hold a Seminar in Your Church

Imagine the results when your church discovers the power of *Would You Like Fries With That?*.

Each year, Mike Silva presents *Would You Like Fries With That?* evangelism training seminars around the country and across the globe. We'd love to receive an invitation for Mike to present one of his next seminars in your area!

It's simple – just send a letter on your church's letterhead to:

Mike Silva
Mike Silva Evangelism, Inc.
P.O. Box 8808
Portland, OR 97207
Phone 503-614-1552
Fax 503-614-1556

In your letter, please let Mike know:

1. How soon would you like to host a seminar?
2. How many people attend your church?
3. Would you like to open up the seminar to other Christians in your community?
4. How many copies of *Would You Like Fries With That?* do you think you need?
5. What length seminar would you like to host?
    ❏ 20- to 40-minute message during main church services
    ❏ 40- to 120-minute seminar for your church (and others)
6. Will the seminar format allow for audience participation?
7. Will the seminar be recorded?

Free Online Resources

You can share some of the artwork and Gospel messages from *Would You Like Fries With That?* with others via e-mail. It's easy! Just log onto www.mikesilva.org and click on "Would You Like Fries With That?." Download one of your favorite illustrations and chapters, then e-mail it to your family and friends.

Here's a suggested note you can adapt and send with each e-mail:

Dear <friend's name>,

Hello again! Say, I just finished reading a great little book by Mike Silva and Matt Williames, illustrator. Their book is called Would You Like Fries With That? *(World Publishing, 2005). You may have seen Matt's work in one of Warner's newest animated feature films. Anyway, I went online to the authors' Web site, where Mike and Matt allow readers to download selected excerpts free of charge. I especially liked their chapter on <title>, which I've attached. Take a look – and then let me know what you think!*

All the best...
<your name>

About the Author and Illustrator

Author **Mike Silva** is one of America's most sought-after evangelists at Creation Festival (East and West), Promise Keepers (each tour), and other large-scale Christian events where the gospel is clearly proclaimed and many thousands trust Jesus Christ each year.

Whether at the nation's largest churches, evangelism conferences, or the National Outreach Convention, Mike Silva is also in demand as an evangelism trainer.

Mike Silva is a frequent guest on *Reaching Your World with Luis Palau* (nearly 900 markets), *Need Him* (more than 1,000 stations), *Prime Time America* (Moody Broadcasting Network), and other popular Christian radio programs.

Mike Silva's evangelistic messages are used as examples of "what works today" by Mark Mittelberg, best-selling author and evangelism trainer; by Dr. Ramesh Richard, evangelism professor at Dallas Theological Seminary; by Dr. Tim Robnett, director, Next Generation Alliance®; and by other nationally known evangelism trainers.

Mike Silva's closest mentors and supporters include world-renowned evangelist Luis Palau, best-selling author and pastor Max Lucado, and other well-known Christian leaders.

After his commitment to Jesus Christ, Mike Silva is devoted to his wife, Crystal, and to his four daughters, Jenna, Delight, Grace, and Kristianna. The Silvas make their home in Oregon.

Illustrator **Matt Williames** is best known for his work on some of Hollywood's most successful new animated feature films, including *Scooby Doo 2: Monsters Unleashed* and *Looney Tunes: Back in Action*. Matt and his wife, Kristin, live in southern California.

About Mike Silva Evangelism

Mike Silva serves as president of Mike Silva Evangelism.

Our mission is to practice and proclaim the life-changing message of the Lord Jesus Christ. In keeping with that mission, we have embraced six core values:

Prayer

Knowing that effective evangelism and conversion depend on God, *not* human effort, we value building this ministry on prayer.

Church-centered

Believing we are part of the church, not a substitute for it, we pledge to engage as many churches and denominations as possible in the initial invitation, preparations, actual outreach event, and follow-up.

Disciples, not decisions

We are committed to making disciples, not decisions, by helping new believers grow spiritually through Bible Study, prayer, witness, and local church integration.

Personal witness

We value a loving, intentional, personal witness. Therefore, we seek to encourage and equip local Christians to be consistent witnesses to the unreached around them and to invite them to our special event.

Volunteer-empowered

Believing that every member of the body of Jesus Christ is a "minister," our goal is to recruit, organize and train large numbers of local Christians to assist in all aspects of our outreach effort.

Pledge of integrity

By applying the highest ethical standards in finance, promotion and follow-up, Mike Silva Evangelism strives to be a leader in ministry and personal integrity.